Better Homes and Gardens®

Hot Off the Grill

© Copyright 1985 by Meredith Corporation, Des Moines, Iowa.
All Rights Reserved. Printed in the United States of America.
First Edition. First Printing.
Library of Congress Catalog Card Number: 84-61310
ISBN: 0-696-01467-X (hard cover)
ISBN: 0-696-01465-3 (trade paperback)

BETTER HOMES AND GARDENS® BOOKS

Editor: Gerald M. Knox
Art Director: Ernest Shelton
Managing Editor: David A. Kirchner

Food and Nutrition Editor: Nancy Byal
Department Head, Cook Books: Sharyl Heiken
Associate Department Heads: Sandra Granseth,
    Rosemary C. Hutchinson, Elizabeth Woolever
Senior Food Editors: Julia Malloy, Marcia Stanley,
    Joyce Trollope
Associate Food Editors: Barbara Atkins, Molly Culbertson,
    Linda Foley, Linda Henry, Lynn Hoppe, Jill Johnson,
    Mary Jo Plutt, Maureen Powers
Recipe Development Editor: Marion Viall
Test Kitchen Director: Sharon Stilwell
Test Kitchen Photo Studio Director: Janet Pittman
Test Kitchen Home Economists: Jean Brekke,
    Kay Cargill, Marilyn Cornelius, Maryellyn Krantz,
    Lynelle Munn, Dianna Nolin, Marge Steenson,
    Cynthia Volcko

Associate Art Directors: Linda Ford Vermie,
    Neoma Alt West, Randall Yontz
Copy and Production Editors: Marsha Jahns,
    Mary Helen Schiltz, Carl Voss, David A. Walsh
Assistant Art Directors: Faith Berven, Harijs Priekulis,
    Tom Wegner
Senior Graphic Designers: Alisann Dixon,
    Lynda Haupert, Lyne Neymeyer
Graphic Designers: Mike Burns, Mike Eagleton,
    Deb Miner, Stan Sams, Darla Whipple-Frain

Vice President, Editorial Director: Doris Eby
Executive Director, Editorial Services: Duane L. Gregg

General Manager: Fred Stines
Director of Publishing: Robert B. Nelson
Vice President, Retail Marketing: Jamie Martin
Vice President, Direct Marketing: Arthur Heydendael

HOT OFF THE GRILL

Editors: Julia Malloy, Mary Jo Plutt
Copy and Production Editor: Mary Helen Schiltz
Graphic Designer: Darla Whipple-Frain
Electronic Text Processor: Donna Russell
Contributing Photographer: Mike Dieter
Food Stylist: Janet Pittman
Contributing Illustrator: Thomas Rosborough

On the cover: Appletom Chicken (see recipe, page 40)

Our seal assures you that every recipe
in *Hot Off the Grill* has been tested in the
Better Homes and Gardens® Test Kitchen.
This means that each recipe is practical
and reliable, and meets our high standards
of taste appeal.

Contents

Maple Chops
(see recipe, page 37)

Vegetable Kabobs
(see recipe, page 91)

Get Fired Up

The road to easier and tastier grilling starts here. Along the way we'll show you how to adapt the basic grilling techniques of yesterday to the fresh new flavor combinations of today.

Start on pages 6 and 7 with the grilling basics. Then look throughout the book for dozens of different ideas to make your barbecue a sizzling success.

Whether you're an expert or just a novice at grilling, our creative recipes, color photographs, and illustrated tip boxes can help you enjoy the fun, flavor, and convenience of barbecuing.

Getting Started

Every successful barbecue begins with one thing—making a successful fire. Before you start your cookout, read through the next two pages and brush up on these fire-making pointers.

● **Choosing a grill.** You'll find a variety of different types of grills on the market. Choose the one that best fits your needs.

Braziers are less-expensive, uncovered grills with shallow fireboxes that are designed for direct cooking only. They have three or four legs and range from simple fold-up units to larger more elaborate units with half-hoods, rotisseries, and air vents.

Hibachis are small, portable grills that are great for directly grilling appetizers and small portions. They come equipped with adjustable grill racks, air vents, and briquette racks to let ashes sift to the bottom.

Kettle and *wagon grills* are larger and more versatile than the braziers or hibachis. Although they differ from brand to brand, they all feature air vents in the bottom and a grill hood to control ventilation. Use both grills for direct and indirect cooking and heat with either charcoal, gas, or electricity.

Water smokers are designed to indirectly cook foods slowly over a fire sprinkled with dampened wood chunks. (See tip box, page 79.)

● **Preparing the firebox.** Cooking with charcoal requires a few more steps in getting the coals ready for cooking than a gas or electric grill.

Check your manufacturer's instructions to see if your charcoal firebox needs to be protected. Protect the firebox by lining it with *heavy* foil and adding an inch of pea gravel or coarse grit. This bed of gravel will allow air in under the briquettes so the coals will burn better. It also protects the firebox from the coals' intense heat and reduces flare-ups by absorbing dripping fats and meat juices. After a dozen uses, change the foil; wash and thoroughly dry the gravel or grit bedding and use again.

● **Determining the amount of briquettes.** As a general rule, estimate the number of briquettes needed by spreading them out into a single layer, extending about an inch beyond the food to be cooked.

On windy and humid days or during longer cooking times, you may find that you'll need a little more charcoal. Also, different brands of briquettes will give off varying degrees of heat. Some brands start slowly but burn a long time. Others start quickly but burn out in a hurry. Only by experimenting will you find the brand that you like best.

● **Lighting the fire.** Pile the briquettes into a pyramid in the center of the firebox. If you're using self-lighting briquettes, simply ignite them with a match. But if you're using standard briquettes, choose one of the starters listed on page 32 to help light the fire.

● **Arranging the coals.** After lighting the fire, leave the briquettes in a pyramid until they look ash gray by day or glow red after dark. Self-lighting briquettes will need to burn about 5 to 10 minutes before they're ready and standard briquettes will need to burn about 20 to 30 minutes.

Once the coals are ready, spread them out for either direct or indirect cooking. The method of cooking you choose will depend on the type of food you're cooking. Check the recipe or the tip box on page 20 to determine which method you'll use.

Direct Cooking

Direct cooking: Use long-handled tongs to spread the hot coals out in a single layer. For a more even heat during cooking, arrange the hot coals about half an inch apart. This also will help to reduce flare-ups caused by fat dripping from the meat onto the coals.

Indirect Cooking

Indirect cooking: Use either a disposable foil drip pan or make your own with *heavy* foil (see illustration on page 22); place the pan in the center of the firebox. Then, using long-handled tongs, arrange the hot coals in a circle around the pan.

● **Judging temperature of the coals.** Just like cooking on a stove, not all foods grill at the same temperature. You can determine the cooking temperature of the coals by holding your hand, palm side down, above the coals at the height your food will be cooked. Then start counting the seconds, "one thousand one, one thousand two." If you need to withdraw your hand after two seconds, the coals are *hot;* after three seconds, they're *medium-hot;* after four seconds, they're *medium;* after five seconds, they're *medium-slow;* and after six seconds, they're *slow.*

Always be sure to check the cooking temperature in the recipe before putting the food on the grill. If you need to adjust the temperature of the coals, check the tip box on page 64.

When cooking with gas or electricity, always check the manufacturer's instructions. These grills have instant starters and the cooking temperature can be controlled by adjusting the setting.

Mix-and-Match Burgers

● In a mixing bowl combine egg and desired liquid. Stir in bread crumbs, desired vegetable, desired condiment, and desired seasoning. Add desired ground meat; mix well.

● Shape the meat mixture into four ¾-inch-thick patties. Place patties in a grill basket, if desired.

● Grill patties, on an uncovered grill, directly over *medium-hot* coals for 7 minutes. Turn and grill to desired doneness, allowing 6 to 10 minutes more for medium. (Grill pork and turkey till well-done.) Brush often with barbecue sauce during the last 10 minutes of grilling.

● Serve patties on hamburger buns. Makes 4 servings.

*Note: If using turkey, brush the cold grill rack or grill basket with cooking oil or spray with a nonstick vegetable spray coating.

If you want something other than a plain old hamburger and don't know what to do, create a new burger combination with our mix-and-match chart. Just select one ingredient from each of the first five columns and combine them with the ingredients from the "All of These" column. With our chart as a guide, you'll be able to mix up an endless array of possibilities.

Liquid	+ Vegetable
2 tablespoons milk	⅓ cup finely chopped onion *or* green onion
2 tablespoons plain yogurt	⅓ cup finely chopped green pepper
2 tablespoons bottled barbecue sauce	⅓ cup finely shredded carrot
2 tablespoons catsup	⅓ cup finely chopped canned mushrooms, drained
2 tablespoons orange juice	¼ cup canned diced green chili peppers, drained

+ **Condiment**	+ **Seasoning**	+ **Meat**	+ **All of These**
2 tablespoons prepared horseradish	2 cloves garlic, minced	1 pound ground beef	1 beaten egg
1 tablespoon prepared mustard	1 tablespoon snipped parsley *or* 1 teaspoon dried parsley flakes	1 pound ground veal	⅓ cup soft bread crumbs
1 tablespoon pickle relish		1 pound ground pork	Bottled barbecue sauce
1 teaspoon Worcester-shire sauce	1 teaspoon chili powder	1 pound ground lamb	4 hamburger buns, split and buttered
1 teaspoon soy sauce	½ teaspoon dried basil, crushed	1 pound ground raw turkey*	
	¼ teaspoon ground ginger		

Great Caesar Burgers

1 2-ounce can anchovy fillets 1 teaspoon Worcestershire sauce Dash pepper 1 pound lean ground beef	● Drain anchovy fillets. Remove 4 fillets; roll up jelly-roll style and set aside. 　　In a medium mixing bowl mash the remaining anchovy fillets. Stir in Worcestershire sauce and pepper. Add ground beef; mix well. Shape meat mixture into four ¾-inch-thick patties. Place in grill basket, if desired.
	● Grill patties, on an uncovered grill, directly over *medium-hot* coals for 6 minutes. Turn and grill to desired doneness, allowing 6 to 9 minutes more for medium.
4 small romaine leaves 8 *or* 12 pieces Caesar Toast (see recipe, far right) 1 tablespoon grated Parmesan cheese 2 tablespoons sliced green onion	● For each serving, place one romaine leaf atop 2 or 3 pieces of Caesar Toast. Top with a meat patty, some of the Parmesan cheese and green onion, and one rolled anchovy fillet. Makes 4 servings.

The toast served with these burgers has the same irresistible seasonings that are used in Caesar salad.

**　　Make *Caesar Toast* by cutting 8 *or* 12 slices of *French bread* ⅛ inch thick. Brush both sides of bread with *olive* or *cooking oil*. Sprinkle with a little *garlic salt*. Place bread slices on a baking sheet. Bake in a 300° oven about 30 minutes or till slices are dry and crisp.**

Keep the Fire Under Control

Fat and meat juices dripping onto hot coals can cause sudden flare-ups. These sudden "blazes" will burn the meat, resulting in a charred flavor. Reduce flare-ups by either raising the grill rack, covering the grill, spacing the hot coals farther apart, or removing a few coals to cut down on the heat. As last resort, remove the food from the grill to prevent it from getting coated with ashes, and mist the fire with a pump-spray bottle filled with water.

Greek Burgers

½ cup soft bread crumbs
½ cup sliced pitted ripe
  olives
⅓ cup dairy sour cream
1 teaspoon dried tarragon,
  crushed
½ teaspoon salt
1 pound ground lamb
	● In a medium mixing bowl combine bread crumbs, ⅓ *cup* of the ripe olives, the ⅓ cup sour cream, tarragon, and salt. Add ground lamb; mix well. Shape meat mixture into four ½-inch-thick patties. Place in a grill basket, if desired.	The all-American burger goes foreign! Lamb, ripe olives, and feta cheese turn this burger into a Mediterranean delicacy.

	● Grill patties, on an uncovered grill, directly over *medium* coals for 6 minutes. Turn and grill to desired doneness, allowing 5 to 6 minutes more for medium.	

⅓ cup cream-style cottage
  cheese
2 tablespoons feta cheese,
  crumbled (½ ounce)
2 tablespoons dairy sour
  cream
	● Meanwhile, in a small mixing bowl combine cottage cheese, feta cheese, the 2 tablespoons sour cream, and the remaining ripe olives.	

4 hamburger buns, split 4 thin tomato slices	● Serve patties on hamburger buns; top with tomato slices and cheese mixture. Makes 4 servings.	

Pita Burgers

¼ cup bulgur wheat
½ cup snipped parsley
2 tablespoons finely
  chopped onion
1 tablespoon dry red wine
1 small clove garlic, minced
½ teaspoon salt
½ teaspoon snipped fresh
  mint *or* ⅛ teaspoon
  dried mint, crushed
¼ teaspoon ground allspice
1 pound ground lamb
	● In a medium mixing bowl cover bulgur with 1 inch of *boiling* water. Let bulgur stand 30 minutes; drain well.
	  Combine the drained bulgur wheat, snipped parsley, finely chopped onion, red wine, minced garlic, salt, mint, and allspice. Add ground lamb; mix well. Shape the meat mixture into four ¾-inch-thick patties. Place the patties in a grill basket, if desired.
		Try a new way of eating a burger—slip it into a "pocket." Depending on your appetite, you can make either large or small pockets. For a smaller serving, cut the pita bread rounds in half; for a larger sandwich, leave the pita whole and slit it partway along the seam. Then slip one burger and some toppings into each pocket.

	● Grill patties, on an uncovered grill, directly over *medium* coals for 6 minutes. Turn and grill to desired doneness, allowing 6 to 9 minutes more for medium.	
2 *or* 4 pita bread rounds Lettuce Chopped cucumber Plain yogurt	● Serve the patties in pita bread with lettuce, chopped cucumber, and yogurt. Makes 4 servings.	

Giant Stuffed Turkey Burger

⅔	**cup water**
⅓	**cup long grain rice**
1	**tablespoon butter** *or* **margarine**
¼	**teaspoon salt**
¼	**teaspoon dried sage, crushed**
⅓	**cup chopped onion**
¼	**cup shredded carrot**
2	**tablespoons snipped parsley**

● For stuffing, in a small saucepan combine water, long grain rice, butter or margarine, the ¼ teaspoon salt, and sage. On the range top, bring mixture to boiling; reduce heat. Cover and simmer for 10 minutes. Stir in chopped onion, carrot, and parsley. Cook, covered, for 5 minutes more. Remove from heat; set rice mixture aside.

2	**pounds ground raw turkey**
	Salt
	Pepper

● Divide meat in half. On two sheets of waxed paper pat each half into a 7-inch circle; sprinkle with salt and pepper.

Spread rice on center of one circle to within ½ inch of edge. Invert second circle atop, as shown at right; peel off top sheet of waxed paper. Press meat around edges to seal.

1	**8-ounce can whole cranberry sauce**
	Green onion (optional)
	Carrot, cut into long, thin strips (optional)

● In a covered grill arrange preheated coals around a drip pan; test for *medium* heat above pan. Invert stuffed burger onto a well-greased grill rack over the drip pan but not over coals; remove waxed paper. Lower grill hood. Grill for 1¼ to 1½ hours or till well-done.

On the range top, heat cranberry sauce. Top burger with the heated cranberry sauce; garnish with green onion and carrot, if desired. Serves 8.

To assemble the burger, spread the rice mixture on the center of one of the meat circles to within ½ inch of the edge. Gently invert and lift the second circle of meat atop filling. Peel off top sheet of waxed paper. Press meat around edges to seal.

Orange-Glazed Ham Patties

⅓ cup orange juice
½ teaspoon cornstarch
⅛ teaspoon ground ginger

● For glaze, in a small saucepan combine orange juice, cornstarch, and ground ginger. On the range top, cook and stir till the orange juice mixture is thickened and bubbly. Cook and stir for 2 minutes more. Set glaze aside.

1 beaten egg
1 tablespoon milk
¾ cup soft bread crumbs
   (1 slice)
2 tablespoons chopped
   onion
1 tablespoon snipped
   parsley
⅛ teaspoon ground ginger
1 pound ground fully
   cooked ham (3 cups)

● In a mixing bowl combine egg and milk. Stir in the soft bread crumbs, chopped onion, snipped parsley, and ground ginger. Add the fully cooked ground ham; mix well.
   Shape the meat mixture into six ¾-inch-thick patties. Place the ham patties in a grill basket, if desired.

● Grill ham patties, on an uncovered grill, directly over *medium-hot* coals for 5 minutes. Turn and brush with the glaze. Grill patties for 5 to 6 minutes more or till heated through.
   Just before serving, brush ham patties with the glaze again. Makes 6 servings.

For indoor grilling, choose recipes with short cooking times, like *Orange-Glazed Ham Patties.* The shorter the time on the grill, the less smoke that needs to be vented. Before doing any grilling inside, check the tips on page 24.

Take-Along Meal

Whether it's a family get-together in the park or a romantic afternoon at the beach, no day outdoors is complete without a meal. This no-fuss picnic is sure to please because it's delicious, easy-to-prepare, light-weight to carry, and requires no messy cleanup. You can't ask for more! (See pages 16 and 17 for recipes.)

MENU

Surprise-Packed Burgers
Whole wheat hamburger buns
Quick Vegetable Relish
Potato chips

Fruit 'n' Honey Apple Slices
Cookies
Lemonade or iced tea

Surprise-Packed Burgers

Pictured on pages 14 and 15.

2 slices bacon	● In a skillet on the range top cook bacon till crisp; drain and crumble.
2 tablespoons thinly sliced green onion 1 tablespoon bottled barbecue sauce, catsup, *or* steak sauce ½ pound ground beef	● In a mixing bowl combine green onion and barbecue sauce, catsup, or steak sauce. Add ground beef; mix well. Shape the meat mixture into four ¼-inch-thick patties.
¼ cup shredded or crumbled Swiss, cheddar, American, mozzarella, Monterey Jack, *or* blue cheese (1 ounce)	● Place *half* of the cheese and crumbled bacon atop *each* of two meat patties. Top with the remaining patties. Press meat around edges to seal. Wrap *each* burger in clear plastic wrap or foil; chill till time to grill.

2 whole wheat hamburger buns, split and buttered	● Unwrap and grill burgers, on an uncovered grill, directly over *medium-hot* coals for 7 minutes. Turn and grill to desired doneness, allowing 6 to 8 minutes more for medium.
	    If desired, toast buns by placing cut surfaces down on the grill rack. Grill for 3 minutes or till toasted.
	    Serve patties on buns. Serves 2.

MENU COUNTDOWN
Before leaving home:
Shape and wrap the Surprise-Packed Burgers; chill. Split, butter, and wrap the whole wheat hamburger buns.
    Prepare the Quick Vegetable Relish and chill.
    Assemble packets of Fruit 'n' Honey Apple Slices.
    Make beverage; put it into an insulated vacuum bottle.
    Pack burgers, relish, and apple packets in an ice-filled insulated chest. Pack barbecue and picnic supplies.
45 minutes ahead:
Light charcoal in grill.
15 minutes ahead:
Unwrap the Surprise-Packed Burgers and grill. Place Fruit 'n' Honey Apple Slices on grill.
3 minutes ahead:
If desired, toast hamburger buns. Pour beverage.

Picnic Safety Pointers

Here are a few tips to help you make sure your picnic food is both safe and delicious.
● Keep hot foods HOT and cold foods COLD. Food held at temperatures between 40° and 140° for a long period of time can spoil easily.
● Pack picnic foods in insulated containers. Preheat or precool insulated vacuum bottles before filling them. To do so, fill the container with hot or cold tap water and cover. After 5 minutes, remove the water and fill.
● Plan picnic menus so there will be no leftovers to spoil. If there are leftovers, place them in an ice-filled insulated chest right after the meal.
● Keep food containers out of the sun. Even in an insulated chest, it's very easy for cold foods to warm up quickly if the container is stored in the hot sunlight.

Quick Vegetable Relish

Pictured on pages 14 and 15.

2 tablespoons Russian salad dressing	● In a small mixing bowl combine the Russian salad dressing and prepared mustard. Add the seeded and chopped cucumber, celery, green pepper, and the finely chopped onion.
1½ teaspoons prepared mustard	
¼ cup chopped, seeded cucumber	
¼ cup chopped celery	Transfer the relish to a covered container and chill till serving time. Serve as a side dish. Makes 2 servings.
¼ cup chopped green pepper	
2 tablespoons finely chopped onion	

Make this relish several hours before serving so the flavors will have time to blend together.

Fruit 'n' Honey Apple Slices

Pictured on pages 14 and 15.

⅓ cup chopped mixed dried fruit *or* **raisins**
¼ teaspoon finely shredded orange peel
3 tablespoons coconut
2 teaspoons honey
¼ teaspoon ground cinnamon

● For the dried fruit mixture, in a mixing bowl combine the chopped mixed dried fruit or raisins and the finely shredded orange peel. Stir in the coconut, honey, and ground cinnamon.

2 medium baking apples
Lemon juice

● Core the apples; slice *each* of the apples into eight rings. Brush the cut surfaces with lemon juice.

Dot apple slices with butter or margarine.

2 tablespoons orange juice
1 tablespoon butter *or* **margarine**

● Cut two 14x12-inch pieces of *heavy* foil. Place *half* of the apple slices in the center of one piece of foil. Sprinkle with *half* of the dried fruit mixture and *1 tablespoon* orange juice. Repeat with the second piece of foil and the remaining apple slices, dried fruit mixture, and orange juice. Dot fruit with butter or margarine, as shown at right.

Bring up the long edges of foil and, leaving a little space for expansion of steam, seal tightly with a double fold. Then fold the short ends to seal, as shown at right.

● Grill foil packets, on an uncovered grill, directly over *medium-hot* coals for 6 minutes. Turn and grill for 6 to 9 minutes more or till heated through. Makes 2 servings.

Wrap apples by bringing up long edges of foil and, leaving room for the expansion of steam, seal with a double fold. Then fold short ends in.

Black-Tie Chuck Steak

1 2- to 3-pound beef chuck steak, cut 1½ inches thick
½ cup red wine vinegar
⅓ cup catsup
1 tablespoon Worcestershire sauce
1 teaspoon sugar
1 teaspoon dried basil, crushed
2 cloves garlic, minced

Mushroom Sauce (see recipe, far right)

● Slash fat edges of steak at 1-inch intervals, being careful not to cut into meat. Place steak in a plastic bag; set in a shallow dish.

For marinade, combine vinegar, catsup, Worcestershire sauce, sugar, basil, and garlic; pour over steak. Close bag. Marinate in refrigerator for 6 hours or overnight, turning bag several times.

Drain steak; set aside ½ cup marinade for Mushroom Sauce. Reserve remaining marinade to brush on steak. Pat excess moisture from steak with paper towels.

● Grill steak, on an uncovered grill, directly over *medium* coals for 15 minutes. Turn and grill to desired doneness, allowing 10 to 15 minutes more for medium. Brush occasionally with marinade during grilling. Serve with Mushroom Sauce. Serves 6 to 8.

Dress up chuck steak or other less-expensive cuts of meat with this tangy Mushroom Sauce. In a saucepan combine the ½ cup marinade; one 4-ounce can *sliced mushrooms*, drained; ¼ cup bias-sliced *green onion*; ¼ cup *sliced pitted ripe olives*; and 2 teaspoons chopped *pimiento*. On the range top cook for 5 to 7 minutes to heat through.

For easier turning, marinate your meat in a plastic bag. Pour the marinade mixture over the meat in the bag. Close the bag; turn it several times.

Peppy Herb Steak

1 2- to 3-pound beef chuck
  steak, cut 1 inch thick
¾ cup dry red wine
½ cup cooking oil
¼ cup lemon juice
2 tablespoons minced
  dried onion
2 tablespoons cracked
  black pepper
2 teaspoons dried thyme,
  crushed
1 teaspoon dried marjoram,
  crushed
¼ teaspoon salt
1 bay leaf

● Slash fat edges of steak at 1-inch intervals, being careful not to cut into meat. Place steak in a plastic bag; set in a shallow dish.

For marinade, in a mixing bowl combine wine, oil, lemon juice, onion, pepper, thyme, marjoram, salt, and bay leaf; pour over the steak in the bag. Close bag. Marinate steak in the refrigerator for 6 hours or overnight, turning the bag several times.

Drain steak, reserving marinade; discard bay leaf. Pat excess moisture from the steak with paper towels.

● Grill the steak, on an uncovered grill, directly over *medium* coals for 9 minutes. Turn and grill to desired doneness, allowing 9 to 11 minutes more for medium. Brush occasionally with the reserved marinade during grilling. Makes 6 to 8 servings.

Before you put on your chef's hat and barbecue apron, make sure you have the cooking utensils you'll need to make grilling safe as well as fun. Use a long-handled basting brush to apply marinades. A brush with a long handle lets you baste the meat without burning your fingers. A long-handled fork, tongs, and pancake turner, as well as heat-resistant mitts, are also helpful accessories that no barbecue chef should be without.

Orange-Soy Steak

1 pound beef round steak,
  cut 1 inch thick
3 tablespoons orange juice
3 tablespoons soy sauce
1 tablespoon dry sherry
¾ teaspoon ground ginger
1 clove garlic, minced

● Trim any excess fat from steak. Place steak in a plastic bag; set the bag in a shallow dish.

For marinade, in a mixing bowl combine orange juice, soy sauce, sherry, ginger, and garlic; pour over steak in bag. Close bag. Marinate steak in the refrigerator for 6 hours or overnight, turning the bag several times.

Drain the steak, reserving the marinade. Pat excess moisture from the steak with paper towels.

You can add an eye-catching garnish to the *Orange-Soy Steak* by making green onion brushes. Trim the ends from green onions. At one or both ends, cut several lengthwise gashes about 2 inches long. Then place the stalks in ice water to crisp and curl. Drain well before serving.

2 teaspoons molasses
2 tablespoons snipped
  parsley

● Stir the molasses into the reserved marinade.

Grill steak, on an uncovered grill, directly over *medium* coals for 9 minutes. Turn and grill to desired doneness, allowing 9 to 11 minutes more for medium. Brush often with the marinade mixture during the last 10 minutes of grilling. Makes 4 servings.

Sherried Honey Ribs

4	**pounds beef plate short ribs, cut into serving-size pieces**
1	**8-ounce can tomato sauce**
½	**cup dry sherry**
¼	**cup honey**
3	**tablespoons brown sugar**
3	**tablespoons soy sauce**
½	**teaspoon garlic powder**
½	**teaspoon ground ginger**

● Place ribs in a large Dutch oven; add enough water to cover. On the range top, bring to boiling; reduce heat. Simmer, covered, about 1½ hours or till meat is tender; drain.

Meanwhile, for marinade, in a mixing bowl combine tomato sauce, sherry, honey, brown sugar, soy sauce, garlic powder, and ginger. Place ribs in a shallow baking dish; pour marinade over ribs. Cover; marinate in the refrigerator for 6 hours or overnight, spooning marinade over ribs several times.

Drain ribs, reserving marinade. Pat moisture from ribs with paper towels.

● In a covered grill arrange preheated coals around a drip pan; test for *slow* heat above pan. Place ribs over drip pan but not over coals. Lower hood. Grill 20 to 25 minutes or till heated through, turning and brushing occasionally with the reserved marinade. Makes 4 servings.

Why do we often recommend marinating foods in a plastic bag placed in a bowl? Because it's less messy and much easier to keep the food covered with the marinade!

To marinate these ribs in a plastic bag rather than in a shallow dish, cool them first before placing them into the bag.

Cooking Over Direct or Indirect Coals

Pairing the type of cooking—direct or indirect—with the kind of meat, poultry, or fish is important to perfect grilling.

● Use the direct cooking method for fast-cooking foods such as steaks, burgers, cut-up poultry, and fish. Grill the food directly over the hot coals or lava rocks. Make sure to watch these foods very closely. The juices that are released during grilling may cause sudden flare-ups. To reduce these flare-ups, follow the suggestions on page 10.

● Use the indirect cooking method for larger cuts of meat, such as roasts, hams, and whole poultry, which require more than 45 minutes of cooking time. Always use a covered grill for indirect cooking. Place meat on the grill rack directly over a foil drip pan with hot coals arranged around the drip pan. Lower the grill hood and use your barbecue as an oven.

Beer-Basted Ribs

3 pounds beef chuck short
   ribs, cut into serving-
   size pieces
1 12-ounce can beer
1 medium onion, chopped
⅓ cup cooking oil
2 tablespoons brown sugar
2 tablespoons chopped
   canned green chili
   peppers, rinsed and
   drained
1 teaspoon dry mustard
½ teaspoon salt

● Place the ribs in a plastic bag; set in a large bowl.

For marinade, in a mixing bowl combine beer, chopped onion, cooking oil, brown sugar, green chili peppers, dry mustard, and salt; pour over the ribs in the bag. Close bag. Marinate the ribs in the refrigerator for 6 hours or overnight, turning bag several times.

Drain the ribs, reserving the marinade. Pat the excess moisture from the ribs with paper towels.

● In a covered grill arrange preheated coals around a drip pan; test for *slow* heat above pan. Place ribs in a rib rack, if desired. Place ribs on grill rack over drip pan but not over coals. Lower grill hood. Grill about 2 hours or till tender, turning and brushing every 30 minutes with the reserved marinade. Before serving, brush ribs with marinade again. Makes 4 servings.

You may not be as familiar with grilled beef ribs as you are with pork ribs, but you'll find that they're just as finger-licking good!

Beef short ribs can be cut from the plate or chuck area, or they can be the ones immediately below the rib steak section. This recipe calls for those from the chuck area because they are meatier than the others.

Sunshine Ribs

3 pounds pork spareribs *or*
   loin back ribs, cut
   into serving-size pieces
½ of a 6-ounce can (⅓ cup)
   frozen pineapple-orange
   juice concentrate,
   thawed
¼ cup water
2 tablespoons cooking oil
1 tablespoon finely
   shredded orange peel
   (optional)
¼ teaspoon pepper

● Place ribs in a plastic bag; set in a large bowl.

For marinade, in a mixing bowl combine the pineapple-orange juice concentrate; water; oil; orange peel, if desired; and pepper. Pour over ribs in bag. Close bag. Marinate ribs in the refrigerator for 6 hours or overnight, turning bag several times.

Drain the ribs, reserving the marinade. Pat the excess moisture from the ribs with paper towels.

● In a covered grill arrange preheated coals around a drip pan; test for *medium-slow* heat above pan. Place ribs in a rib rack, if desired. Place ribs on grill rack over drip pan but not over coals. Lower grill hood. Grill about 1¼ hours or till no pink remains, turning and brushing ribs every 30 minutes with the reserved marinade. Makes 4 servings.

Don't peek! When cooking in a covered grill, your grill acts like an oven. And just like an oven, if you open it up too often the ribs will take longer to cook.

Peking Pork

1 4½- to 5-pound boneless pork top loin roast (double loin, tied)
¼ cup soy sauce
¼ cup dry sherry
2 tablespoons brown sugar
1 clove garlic, minced
½ teaspoon aniseed, crushed
⅛ teaspoon pepper

● Trim any excess fat from roast. Pierce roast in several places with a long-tine fork. Place roast in a large plastic bag; set in a shallow dish.

For marinade, in a mixing bowl combine soy sauce, sherry, brown sugar, garlic, aniseed, and pepper; pour over roast in bag. Close bag. Marinate in the refrigerator for 6 hours or overnight, turning bag several times.

Drain roast, reserving marinade. Pat moisture from roast with paper towels.

Let the aroma of *Peking Pork* transport you from your own backyard to romantic China. The subtle anise seasoning of this roast is reminiscent of many Chinese dishes. The secret to its wonderful flavor is piercing the meat so it will soak up the soy-sherry marinade.

● Insert meat thermometer near center of roast. In a covered grill arrange preheated coals around a drip pan; test for *medium* heat above pan. Place roast on rack over drip pan but not over coals. Lower hood. Grill for 2 to 2½ hours or till thermometer registers 170°, brushing occasionally with the reserved marinade during the last 30 to 45 minutes of grilling. Makes 10 servings.

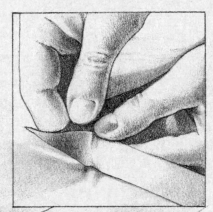

For indirect grilling, use a foil drip pan to catch juices and fat that fall from the meat.

You can buy disposable foil pans at the supermarket. Or, make your own: Tear off a piece of 18-inch-wide *heavy* foil twice the length of your grill; fold it in half for a double thickness. Turn edges up 1½ inches. Miter corners by pressing the tips of the corners together and folding them toward the inside.

Tangy Chops

4 pork loin rib chops, cut ½ inch thick
¼ cup cooking oil
¼ cup cider vinegar
2 cloves garlic, minced
1 teaspoon dried rosemary, crushed
¼ teaspoon crushed red pepper

● Place pork chops in a shallow dish. For marinade, in a mixing bowl combine cooking oil, cider vinegar, minced garlic, rosemary, and crushed red pepper; pour over pork chops in the dish. Turn chops to coat with marinade. Cover and marinate in the refrigerator for 6 hours or overnight, turning the pork chops several times.
  Drain the pork chops, reserving the marinade. Pat excess moisture from chops with paper towels.

Marinate these chops in a cider vinegar mixture to give them a tangy flavor.

● Grill pork chops, on an uncovered grill, directly over *medium-hot* coals for 5 minutes; turn and brush with the reserved marinade. Grill for 5 to 7 minutes more or till no pink remains. Makes 4 servings.

Chicken Sate

1 2½- to 3-pound broiler-fryer chicken, cut up
¼ cup prepared mustard
¼ cup honey
2 tablespoons creamy peanut butter
  Several dashes of bottled hot pepper sauce

● Place chicken pieces in a shallow dish. For marinade, in a mixing bowl combine mustard, honey, peanut butter, and hot pepper sauce; pour over chicken in the dish. Turn chicken pieces to coat with marinade. Cover and marinate chicken in the refrigerator for 6 hours or overnight, turning chicken several times.
  Remove the chicken pieces from the marinade, reserving marinade.

Traditionally, sate (SAH-tay) refers to kabobs served with a spicy-hot peanut sauce. We've adapted the flavors from the sauce to marinate chicken.

● In a covered grill arrange preheated coals around a drip pan; test for *medium* heat above pan. Place chicken pieces on grill rack over drip pan but not over coals. Lower grill hood. Grill for 45 to 55 minutes or till tender, brushing chicken pieces occasionally with the reserved marinade during grilling. Makes 6 servings.

Barbecued Salmon Steaks

4 fresh _or_ frozen salmon steaks, cut 1- to 1¼-inches thick (about 2 pounds) **¼ cup cooking oil** **¼ cup orange juice** **¼ cup dry white wine** **3 tablespoons snipped parsley** **2 cloves garlic, minced** **¼ teaspoon salt** **Dash pepper**	● Thaw salmon, if frozen. Place salmon in a shallow dish. For marinade, in a small mixing bowl combine cooking oil, orange juice, white wine, parsley, garlic, salt, and pepper; pour over salmon in the dish. Turn salmon to coat with marinade. Cover and marinate salmon in the refrigerator for 6 hours or overnight, turning the salmon several times. Drain salmon, reserving the marinade. Pat the excess moisture from the salmon with paper towels.
Lemon wedges (optional)	● Grill salmon, on an uncovered grill, directly over _medium-hot_ coals for 7 minutes. Turn and grill for 6 to 8 minutes more or till salmon flakes easily when tested with a fork, brushing occasionally with the reserved marinade. If desired, serve with lemon wedges. Makes 4 servings.

Bring Outdoor Grilling Inside

You can safely bring the spirit and good flavors of outdoor grilling inside by following these few tips:
● Check manufacturer's instructions to see if your grill can be used inside.
● Choose foods which require only a short cooking time. This keeps smoke to a minimum.
● Natural gas and electric grills are commonly used for indoor grilling. These grills are permanently installed. Never use portable propane grills indoors.
● Charcoal grills can be used in the back of a fireplace with the damper or flue open.
● Charcoal gives off toxic fumes as it burns, so make sure the smoke and fumes go

directly up the chimney. After you've finished cooking, leave the coals in the fireplace until they burn out. Or, if you have a covered grill, put them out by closing the vents. Never try to transport hot coals to another area because the ashes may fall and cause a fire.
● The key to any indoor grilling is adequate ventilation. Whether you're using a portable grill in the back of your fireplace or a grill that's permanently installed, make sure the ventilation system is powerful enough to exhaust the fumes outdoors.

Creole Roast

2 to 2½ pounds beef tenderloin
1 tablespoon Worcestershire sauce

● Trim any excess fat from meat. Rub Worcestershire sauce over surface of meat with your fingers.

---

1 tablespoon snipped parsley *or* 1 teaspoon dried parsley flakes
½ teaspoon salt
½ teaspoon pepper
¼ teaspoon celery seed
⅛ to ¼ teaspoon ground red pepper
⅛ teaspoon onion powder
⅛ teaspoon garlic powder
⅛ teaspoon ground cloves

● In a custard cup combine parsley, salt, pepper, celery seed, red pepper, onion powder, garlic powder, and ground cloves. Sprinkle the spice mixture over meat; rub in with your fingers. Cover roast and let stand at room temperature for 1 hour or overnight in the refrigerator.

● In a covered grill arrange preheated coals around a drip pan; test for *medium* heat above the pan. Insert a meat thermometer near center of roast. Place roast on grill rack over pan but not over coals. Lower hood. Grill till thermometer registers 140° for rare (about 45 minutes), 160° for medium (about 55 minutes), and 170° for well-done (about 1 hour). Makes 6 to 8 servings.

Use either a covered grill or a rotisserie accessory to cook this Southern-flavored roast. For the rotisserie method, insert the spit rod lengthwise through center of roast. Adjust holding forks; test balance. Insert a meat thermometer near center of roast, not touching spit rod. Attach spit to grill; turn motor on. Grill roast, on an uncovered grill, directly over *medium* coals to desired doneness, using the times at left.

Rotisserie Cooking

A great way to get juicy, evenly cooked foods is to use a rotisserie. The secret to the delicious results is that the meat or poultry bastes itself as it turns.

For best results, make sure the food is balanced on the spit. Insert the spit rod lengthwise through the center of the meat or poultry and secure it with the holding forks. To test the balance, hold the ends of the rod in the palms of your hands and rotate the rod gently. If the meat flops or turns unevenly, readjust the holding forks or the spit rod as necessary and retest the balance.

In our recipes, we use an uncovered grill and cook with direct heat. But if you have a covered grill with a rotisserie accessory, you can use either direct or indirect heat for cooking. (See pages 6 and 7.)

Curried Beef Ribs

3 **pounds beef chuck short ribs** **Water** 1 **lemon, cut into quarters**	● Place ribs in a large Dutch oven; add water to cover. Add lemon quarters. On the range top, bring to boiling; reduce heat. Simmer, covered, about 1½ hours or till meat is tender. Drain; let stand till cool enough to handle.
2 **tablespoons butter** *or* **margarine** 1 **tablespoon sugar** 1 **teaspoon cracked black pepper** 1 **teaspoon ground cinnamon** ½ **teaspoon ground cumin** ½ **teaspoon ground cardamom** ¼ **teaspoon salt** ¼ **teaspoon ground cloves** ⅛ **teaspoon ground nutmeg** ⅛ **teaspoon ground turmeric**	● Meanwhile, in a saucepan on the range top melt the 2 tablespoons butter or margarine; stir in sugar, pepper, cinnamon, cumin, cardamom, salt, cloves, nutmeg, and turmeric. Cook over low heat till sugar is just dissolved. Cool. Rub mixture over ribs with your fingers. In a covered grill arrange preheated coals around a drip pan; test for *slow* heat above pan. Place ribs in rib rack, if desired. Place ribs on grill rack over pan but not over coals. Lower hood. Grill for 20 to 25 minutes or till heated through.
¼ **cup sliced green onion** 1 **tablespoon butter** *or* **margarine** 1 **medium tomato, seeded and chopped** 2 **tablespoons snipped fresh cilantro** *or* **parsley** 1 **tablespoon honey** ½ **cup plain yogurt**	● For sauce, in a pan on the range top cook onion in the 1 tablespoon butter or margarine till tender but not brown. Stir in tomato, cilantro or parsley, and honey. Remove from heat; stir in yogurt. Serve with ribs. Makes 4 servings.

For this recipe, combine several ground spices together to make a one-of-a-kind homemade curry blend. Our Test Kitchen has found that the key to "unlocking" and blending the flavors is to cook the spices in a small amount of butter.

Jars labeled *aniseed*, *dillseed*, *fennel seed*

Seeded Roast

1   3½-pound boneless pork
     top loin roast
3   tablespoons soy sauce
2   tablespoons aniseed
2   tablespoons fennel seed
2   tablespoons caraway seed
2   tablespoons dillseed

● Trim any excess fat from roast; rub soy sauce over surface with your fingers. In a 15x10x1-inch baking pan combine aniseed, fennel, caraway, and dillseed. Roll meat in seeds to coat evenly, as shown at right. Wrap meat in foil; let stand in the refrigerator for 1 to 2 hours or overnight.

Remove foil. Insert meat thermometer near center of roast. In a covered grill arrange preheated coals around a drip pan; test for *medium* heat above pan. Place roast on rack over drip pan but not over coals. Lower grill hood. Grill for 2 to 2½ hours or till thermometer registers 170°. Serves 12 to 14.

● **Rotisserie method:** Insert spit rod lengthwise through center of roast. Adjust holding forks; test balance. Insert meat thermometer near center of roast, not touching spit rod. Attach spit to grill; turn motor on. Grill roast, on an uncovered grill, directly over *medium* coals for 2 to 2½ hours or till meat thermometer registers 170°.

Add flavor and crunch to the outside of your pork roast by rolling it in four kinds of seeds. Combine the seeds in a 15x10x1-inch baking pan. Roll the roast in the seeds to coat it evenly. If necessary, press the seeds onto the surface of the roast to make them stick.

Spiced Pork Chops

Gingerroot (see tip, far right)	● Peel the skin from the gingerroot. Rub the peeled gingerroot over the surface of both sides of each pork chop.
4 pork loin chops, cut ½ inch thick	
1 tablespoon soy sauce	Brush chops with soy sauce.

½ teaspoon paprika	● In a custard cup combine paprika, dry mustard, and pepper. Sprinkle the spice mixture over the pork chops; rub in with your fingers.
¼ teaspoon dry mustard	
¼ teaspoon pepper	
	Grill pork chops, on an uncovered grill, directly over *medium-hot* coals for 5 minutes. Turn and grill for 5 to 7 minutes more or till no pink remains. Makes 4 servings.

You'll need only a small amount of gingerroot. Just cut off one or two ¼-inch-thick slices and peel. Wrap and freeze the remaining unpeeled gingerroot for other uses.

Citrus Chicken

½ teaspoon finely shredded orange, lemon, *or* lime peel (set aside)	● Squeeze and rub the cut surface of the orange, lemon, or lime halves over the chicken pieces.
1 medium orange, lemon, *or* lime, cut in half	
1 2½- to 3-pound broiler-fryer chicken, cut up	

1 teaspoon sugar	● In a custard cup combine the finely shredded peel, sugar, salt, ground cinnamon, and red pepper. Sprinkle the peel mixture over the chicken pieces; rub in with your fingers.
½ teaspoon salt	
¼ teaspoon ground cinnamon	
⅛ teaspoon ground red pepper	

	● Grill chicken pieces with bone side up, on an uncovered grill, directly over *medium* coals for 20 minutes. Turn and grill for 10 to 20 minutes more or till tender. Makes 4 servings.

Does citrus strike your fancy? You can choose either orange, lemon, or lime to flavor this chicken. Or, use this rub to flavor Cornish game hens. Cut two 1- to 1½-pound hens in half and prepare them as you would the chicken.

Place the roast on a cutting board with bone side down. Cut about four slits, 1½ inches apart and 1 inch deep.

After cutting the slits in the roast, brush the surface with cooking oil.

Release the flavor of the dried herbs by crushing them with a mortar and pestle. Sprinkle the herb mixture over the meat. With your fingers, rub the herbs into the surface of the meat, pressing them into the slits.

Herbed Lamb

1 1½- to 1¾-pound lamb rib roast (8 to 10 ribs)
1 tablespoon cooking oil
½ teaspoon salt
½ teaspoon dried thyme, crushed
½ teaspoon dried rosemary, crushed
½ teaspoon dried savory, crushed
¼ teaspoon pepper

Fresh herbs (optional)

● Trim any excess fat from roast. On top side of roast, cut slits 1½ inches apart and 1 inch deep.

Brush surface of meat with oil.

In a small dish combine salt, thyme, rosemary, savory, and pepper. Sprinkle mixture over the meat; rub in with your fingers, pressing herbs into the slits.

Insert a meat thermometer near center of roast, not touching bone.

● In a covered grill arrange preheated coals around a drip pan; test for *medium* heat above the pan. Place roast with bone side down on the grill rack over drip pan but not over coals. Lower grill hood. Grill till meat thermometer registers 160° for medium (about 1 hour) or to desired doneness.

If desired, garnish with fresh herbs. Makes 4 to 5 servings.

It's the savory blend of herbs that gives this lamb roast its flavor. You can either crush the dried herbs by using a mortar and pestle, as we did, or just rub them between your fingers.

To serve, carve the lamb into rib portions.

Garlic Chicken

1 2½- to 3-pound broiler-fryer chicken
1 large clove garlic, cut in half

● Rinse chicken; pat excess moisture from chicken with paper towels. Rub cut edges of the garlic halves over the outside and inside of the chicken; leave garlic inside of chicken.

¼ teaspoon salt
¼ teaspoon poultry seasoning
⅛ teaspoon ground red pepper

● In a small mixing bowl combine salt, poultry seasoning, and red pepper. Sprinkle the seasoning mixture over the outside of the chicken; rub in with your fingers. Skewer neck skin to back of chicken. Tie legs to tail with cord. Twist the wing tips under the back.

● In a covered grill arrange preheated coals around a drip pan; test for *medium* heat above the pan. Place chicken, breast side up, on a grill rack over the drip pan but not over the coals. Lower grill hood. Grill for 55 to 65 minutes or till a drumstick moves easily in its socket. Makes 6 servings.

If your grill has a rotisserie, you can twirl this bird to golden perfection with these simple directions. Skewer neck skin to back. Insert spit rod lengthwise through chicken. Tie a piece of cord around chicken to prevent legs and wings from flopping. Adjust holding forks; test balance. Attach the spit to the highest setting on the grill; turn motor on. Grill, on an uncovered grill, directly over *medium* coals for 1¼ to 1½ hours or till a drumstick moves easily in its socket.

Fast Fire Starters

With a flick of a match, and one of these starters, you can get a fire going in your grill lickety-split.
● Standard charcoal starters are available in either a liquid or jelly form. Be sure to allow the liquid or jelly to soak into the briquettes for about a minute before lighting and don't add more once the fire is going. Never use gasoline or kerosene. Gasoline may explode and kerosene adds an unpleasant taste.
● Electric starters provide glowing coals in only 5 to 15 minutes. Pile the briquettes over the starter coil and plug in the starter. When the coals are ready, remove the coil and put it in a safe, heat-proof place.
● A chimney-type starter is another fast way to light charcoal. Just load the cylinder with newspaper and briquettes and light the newspaper. The fire from the newspaper will soon light the charcoal.

Fillets with Horseradish Rub

1 pound fresh *or* frozen fish fillets *or* fish steaks *or* two 8-ounce pan-dressed fish	● Thaw fish, if frozen. Cut large fillets or steaks into four equal portions; leave pan-dressed fish whole. Pat excess moisture from fish with paper towels.
2 tablespoons butter *or* margarine, softened 2 tablespoons prepared horseradish 1 tablespoon snipped chives 1 teaspoon snipped fresh dill *or* ¼ teaspoon dillweed ⅛ teaspoon pepper	● In a small mixing bowl combine the softened butter or margarine and prepared horseradish. Stir in snipped chives, dill, and pepper. Rub the horseradish mixture over all sides of the fish and inside the cavities of the pan-dressed fish with your fingers. Cover the fish and let stand in the refrigerator for 30 minutes.
	● Place fish into a well-greased wire grill basket. Grill fish, on an uncovered grill, directly over *medium-hot* coals for 8 minutes. Turn and grill for 8 to 12 minutes more or till the fish flakes easily when tested with a fork, as shown below. Makes 4 servings.

Don't let technical "fish talk" confuse you. A quick reading of these terms will take the guesswork out of shopping.

Fillets are boneless pieces cut lengthwise from the sides of the fish.

Steaks are crosswise slices with only a cross-section of the backbone left in.

Pan-dressed fish are small whole fish that have been cleaned out and scaled. The head, tail, and fins usually have been removed too.

To test fish for doneness, insert the fork tines into the flesh at a 45-degree angle. Twist the fork gently. The fish will be done if it flakes easily.

Spicy Barbecue Sauce

1	10¾-ounce can condensed tomato soup
½	cup water
½	cup finely chopped onion
1	4-ounce can diced green chili peppers, drained
2	tablespoons steak sauce
2	teaspoons chili powder
½	teaspoon sugar
⅛	teaspoon garlic powder
⅛	teaspoon pepper
	Several dashes bottled hot pepper sauce

● In a medium saucepan combine the tomato soup, water, onion, green chili peppers, steak sauce, chili powder, sugar, garlic powder, pepper, and hot pepper sauce. On the range top, bring mixture to boiling; reduce heat. Cover and simmer mixture for 15 minutes.

Brush onto burgers, chicken, or ribs during the last 15 minutes of grilling.

Store, tightly covered, in refrigerator for up to 2 weeks. Makes 2½ cups.

For a barbecue sauce that's fiery hot, simply dash in more bottled hot pepper sauce.

Mustard Sauce

3	tablespoons water
2	tablespoons dry mustard
1	teaspoon cornstarch
3	tablespoons light corn syrup
1	tablespoon vinegar
¼	teaspoon dried tarragon *or* basil, crushed

● In a small saucepan combine water, dry mustard, and cornstarch. Stir in corn syrup, vinegar, and tarragon or basil. On the range top, cook and stir over medium heat till thickened and bubbly. Cook and stir for 2 minutes more.

Brush often onto sausages, burgers, or pork during the last 5 minutes of grilling.

Store, tightly covered, in refrigerator for up to 2 weeks. Makes ⅓ cup.

Mustard Sauce

Spicy Barbecue Sauce

Picanté Sauce

2½ cups cherry tomatoes *or*
   3 medium tomatoes,
   cut up
 1 medium onion, cut up
 1 to 2 cloves garlic
 2 fresh medium jalapeño
   peppers *or* hot red
   peppers, seeded
 1 medium green pepper,
   finely chopped
 ½ cup vinegar
 1 teaspoon salt
 1 teaspoon sugar
 ¼ teaspoon dried oregano,
   crushed
   Dash ground red
   pepper
   Dash ground cumin

● Place unpeeled tomatoes in a blender container or food processor bowl; cover and blend till coarsely ground. Add onion, garlic, and jalapeño or hot red peppers; cover and blend till finely ground. Stir in green pepper.

Transfer mixture to a medium saucepan. Stir in vinegar, salt, sugar, oregano, ground red pepper, and cumin. On the range top, bring to boiling; reduce heat. Simmer, uncovered, for 30 to 40 minutes or to desired consistency.

Brush often onto ribs or burgers during the last 15 minutes of grilling.

Store, tightly covered, in refrigerator for up to 2 weeks. Makes 2⅔ cups.

The hotness in this sauce comes from the jalapeño peppers. These peppers contain oils which can burn your skin and especially your eyes. To be safe, wear rubber gloves while handling the hot peppers and avoid touching your eyes. After you're finished, wash your hands thoroughly.

Sweet-Sour Sauce

 2 tablespoons butter *or*
   margarine
 ½ cup catsup
 ½ cup honey
 ⅓ cup frozen orange juice
   concentrate
 2 tablespoons lemon juice
 2 tablespoons soy sauce
 ½ teaspoon ground ginger

● In a saucepan on the range top melt butter or margarine. Stir in catsup, honey, orange juice, lemon juice, soy sauce, and ginger. Bring to boiling; reduce heat. Simmer mixture, uncovered, for 5 minutes.

Brush often onto meat, poultry, or fish during the last 5 minutes of grilling.

Store, tightly covered, in refrigerator for up to 2 weeks. Makes 1½ cups.

Sweet-Sour Sauce

Picanté Sauce

Savory Grilled Steak

½ cup tomato sauce
1 tablespoon brown sugar
1 tablespoon Worcester-
shire sauce
1 tablespoon finely chopped
onion
1 clove garlic, minced
¼ teaspoon ground nutmeg
⅛ teaspoon ground
cinnamon
⅛ teaspoon pepper

● For the sauce, in a small saucepan combine tomato sauce, brown sugar, Worcestershire sauce, finely chopped onion, minced garlic, ground nutmeg, ground cinnamon, and pepper. On the range top, bring the mixture to boiling; reduce heat. Simmer, uncovered, for 5 minutes; remove from heat.

1 1½-pound beef
porterhouse steak,
or one 2-pound beef
sirloin steak, cut
1½ inches thick

● Grill the steak, on an uncovered grill, directly over *medium-hot* coals for 10 minutes. Turn and brush once with the sauce. Continue grilling to desired doneness, allowing 10 to 12 minutes more for medium.

4 canned pineapple slices,
drained

● During the last 5 minutes of grilling, place the pineapple slices alongside the steak and grill, brushing frequently with the sauce. Heat any remaining sauce on the side of the grill.

● Transfer steak and pineapple to a heated serving platter. Brush steak with sauce again. To serve, slice steak across the grain; pass with the remaining heated sauce. Makes 4 servings.

You can be a pro at judging the doneness of grilled steaks. Just make a small slit in the center of the steak and note the inside color: red—rare; pink—medium; gray— well-done.

Maple Chops

Pictured on page 4 and 5.

1 cup maple-flavored syrup
1 cup catsup
¾ cup dry white wine
¼ cup water
2 cloves garlic, minced
1 bay leaf
1 teaspoon instant beef
    bouillon granules
1 teaspoon grated
    gingerroot
1 teaspoon dried thyme,
    crushed
1 teaspoon dried basil,
    crushed
½ teaspoon salt
½ teaspoon dry mustard
½ teaspoon chili powder
¼ teaspoon pepper
⅛ teaspoon ground cloves
4 pork loin rib chops, cut
    1½ inches thick

● For the sauce, in a small saucepan combine the maple-flavored syrup, catsup, white wine, water, garlic, bay leaf, beef bouillon, ginger, thyme, basil, salt, dry mustard, chili powder, pepper, and cloves. On the range top, bring to boiling; reduce heat. Simmer, uncovered, for 30 minutes or till mixture is reduced to about 2 cups, stirring occasionally.

Grill chops, on an uncovered grill, directly over *medium* coals for 25 minutes. Turn and grill for 20 to 25 minutes more or till no pink remains, brushing often with the sauce during the last 10 minutes of grilling. Heat the remaining sauce on the side of the grill to pass with the chops. Makes 4 servings.

We tested this maple sauce recipe on thick pork loin rib chops. If you would rather use thinner chops, grill ½-inch *pork loin chops,* on an uncovered grill, directly over *medium-hot* coals for 5 minutes. Turn and grill for 5 to 7 minutes more or till no pink remains, brushing often with the maple sauce during the last 5 minutes of grilling.

Country Ribs

4 pounds pork country-style
    ribs
  Salt
  Pepper

● Place ribs in a large Dutch oven; add enough water to cover. Bring to boiling; reduce heat. Simmer, covered, for 45 to 60 minutes or till meat is tender; drain. Sprinkle ribs with salt and pepper.

Company coming? Precook the ribs and make the apple butter sauce a day ahead. Then store the ribs and sauce in the refrigerator until you're ready to grill.

1 14-ounce jar apple butter
½ cup water
¼ cup vinegar
3 tablespoons lemon juice
2 teaspoons prepared
    horseradish
1 teaspoon prepared
    mustard
½ teaspoon sugar
½ teaspoon salt
½ teaspoon garlic powder
½ teaspoon celery seed
⅛ teaspoon pepper
  Dash ground red pepper
  Dash ground cumin

● For the sauce, in a saucepan combine apple butter, water, vinegar, lemon juice, horseradish, mustard, sugar, the ½ teaspoon salt, garlic powder, celery seed, the ⅛ teaspoon pepper, red pepper, and cumin. On the range top, bring to boiling; reduce heat. Simmer, uncovered, for 25 minutes or till mixture is reduced to about 2 cups, stirring occasionally.

● Place the ribs in a rib rack, if desired. Grill the ribs, on an uncovered grill, directly over *slow* coals about 45 minutes or till heated through, turning every 15 minutes. Brush ribs often with the sauce during the last 15 minutes of grilling. Makes 4 to 6 servings.

Red Hot Spareribs

1 15-ounce can tomato
   sauce
¼ cup packed brown sugar
¼ cup red wine vinegar
2 tablespoons Worcester-
   shire sauce
2 tablespoons prepared
   mustard
1 tablespoon chili powder
1½ teaspoons celery seed
¼ to ½ teaspoon ground red
   pepper

● For the sauce, in a small saucepan combine the tomato sauce, brown sugar, red wine vinegar, Worcestershire sauce, prepared mustard, chili powder, celery seed, and ground red pepper. On the range top, bring mixture to boiling; reduce heat. Simmer, uncovered, for 10 minutes; set sauce aside.

Calling all hot and spicy lovers—this one's for you! For juicy ribs, first cook the ribs slowly in a covered grill. Then for easy basting, take the cover off during the last 15 minutes of grilling.

4 pounds pork spareribs
   or pork loin back ribs,
   cut into serving-size
   pieces

● In a covered grill arrange preheated coals around a drip pan; test for *medium* heat above the pan. Place ribs in a rib rack, if desired. Place ribs on grill rack over drip pan but not over coals. Lower grill hood. Grill for 25 minutes. Turn and grill, covered, for 20 minutes more.

● Brush sauce onto both sides of ribs. Continue grilling the ribs, on an *uncovered* grill, about 15 minutes more or till no pink remains. Brush occasionally with the sauce.

● Heat any of the remaining sauce on the side of the grill to pass with ribs. Makes 4 to 6 servings.

Tangy Chicken

¼ cup catsup
2 tablespoons soy sauce
1 tablespoon cooking oil
1 tablespoon lemon juice
1 tablespoon prepared
    horseradish

● For sauce, in a small mixing bowl combine catsup, soy sauce, cooking oil, lemon juice, and prepared horseradish.

We tested this chicken in a covered grill, but you can also cook it on an uncovered grill—just add 5 to 10 minutes more to the grilling time.

4 chicken legs

● Grill chicken, in a covered grill, directly over *medium* coals for 15 minutes. Turn and grill for 15 to 25 minutes more or till tender, brushing often with sauce during the last 10 minutes of grilling. Makes 4 servings.

Appletom Chicken

½ cup finely chopped onion
2 cloves garlic, minced
2 tablespoons cooking oil
1 14½-ounce can whole
    peeled tomatoes, finely
    cut up
¼ cup vinegar
2 tablespoons brown sugar
½ teaspoon dried tarragon,
    crushed
¼ teaspoon ground red
    pepper
⅛ teaspoon pepper
1 8-ounce can unsweetened
    applesauce

● For sauce, in a medium saucepan on the range top cook onion and garlic in cooking oil till onion is tender but not brown. Stir in *undrained* tomatoes, vinegar, brown sugar, tarragon, red pepper, and pepper. Bring to boiling; reduce heat. Boil gently, uncovered, for 25 to 30 minutes or to desired consistency, stirring occasionally.
　Stir in the applesauce and heat through. Set sauce aside.

Pictured at right and on the cover.

Apple and tomato add a new appeal to classic barbecued chicken. Also try this chunky apple-tomato sauce on pork, beef, or fish.

6 chicken legs

● Grill chicken, in a covered grill, directly over *medium* coals for 15 minutes. Turn and grill for 15 to 25 minutes more or till tender, brushing often with the sauce during the last 10 minutes of grilling.
　Heat any remaining sauce on the side of the grill to pass with the chicken. Makes 6 servings.

Appletom Chicken

Manhattan-Style Chicken

1   6½-ounce can minced
    clams
1   8-ounce bottle (1 cup)
    clam juice
1   cup catsup
1   small onion, finely
    chopped (¼ cup)
1   clove garlic, minced
2   tablespoons cooking oil
1   tablespoon Worcester-
    shire sauce
½   teaspoon finely shredded
    lemon peel (optional)
1   tablespoon lemon juice
2   tablespoons snipped
    parsley

● Drain the clams, reserving the liquid. Set clams aside.

For the sauce, in a medium saucepan combine the reserved clam liquid; clam juice; catsup; finely chopped onion; minced garlic; cooking oil; Worcestershire sauce; the finely shredded lemon peel, if desired; and lemon juice. On the range top, bring the mixture to boiling and reduce heat. Simmer, uncovered, for 30 to 35 minutes or to desired consistency. Remove the mixture from the heat; stir in the minced clams and snipped parsley.

1   2½- to 3-pound broiler-
    fryer chicken, cut up

● Grill chicken pieces with bone side up, on an uncovered grill, directly over *medium* coals for 20 minutes. Turn and grill 10 to 20 minutes more or till tender, brushing often with sauce during the last 10 minutes of grilling.

Heat any of the remaining sauce on the side of the grill to pass with the chicken. Makes 6 servings.

We based the recipe for this chicken on a Manhattan clam chowder. The sauce gives this chicken its golden-red color and clam flavor.

For a more attractive chicken, first grill the chicken pieces with the bone side up. Then, when you turn the chicken over, it will be easier to brush the sauce onto the meaty side.

Lemony Chicken

¼   teaspoon finely shredded
    lemon peel
¼   cup lemon juice
1   tablespoon brown sugar
1   tablespoon snipped
    parsley
1   tablespoon cooking oil
1   clove garlic, minced
¼   teaspoon dried oregano,
    crushed
¼   teaspoon salt
    Dash pepper

● For the lemon sauce, in a small mixing bowl combine the finely shredded lemon peel, lemon juice, brown sugar, snipped parsley, cooking oil, minced garlic, oregano, salt, and pepper.

Avoid flare-ups by brushing the lemon sauce on the chicken after you turn it. This way, only a small amount of the sauce will drip onto the hot coals.

1   2½- to 3-pound broiler-
    fryer chicken, halved
    lengthwise

● Break wing, hip, and drumstick joints of chicken; twist wing tips under back.

Grill chicken halves with bone side up, on an uncovered grill, directly over *medium-hot* coals for 20 minutes. Turn and grill for 25 to 30 minutes more or till tender, brushing often with the lemon sauce during the last 5 to 10 minutes of grilling. Makes 6 servings.

Grilled Rabbit

1 6-ounce can frozen apple juice concentrate, thawed
¼ cup packed brown sugar
¼ cup catsup
1 tablespoon vinegar
Several drops bottled hot pepper sauce

● For the sauce, in a small saucepan combine the apple juice concentrate, brown sugar, catsup, vinegar, and hot pepper sauce. On the range top, heat and stir the mixture till sugar dissolves.

Look for rabbit in a specialty meat shop or in the supermarket. Or, substitute a chicken. The flavor of rabbit is often compared to chicken.

1 2- to 2½-pound rabbit *or* one 2½- to 3-pound broiler-fryer chicken, cut up
Salt
Pepper
Cooking oil

● Sprinkle rabbit or chicken with salt and pepper. Grill rabbit or chicken pieces with bone side up, on an uncovered grill, directly over *medium* coals for 20 minutes. Turn and brush pieces with oil. Continue grilling for 10 to 20 minutes more or till tender, brushing often with the sauce during the last 5 minutes of grilling. Transfer the rabbit or chicken pieces to a warm platter and keep warm.

1 tablespoon cold water
2 teaspoons cornstarch

● Add enough water to the remaining sauce to make 1 cup. Combine the 1 tablespoon cold water and cornstarch; stir into sauce mixture. On the range top, cook and stir till thickened and bubbly. Cook 2 minutes more. Pass sauce with rabbit or chicken. Makes 6 servings.

Salmon with Caper Butter

4 fresh *or* frozen salmon steaks, cut 1 inch thick (about 2 pounds)
1 tablespoon capers, drained
2 tablespoons butter *or* margarine, softened
¼ teaspoon dried fines herbes, crushed

● Thaw the salmon, if frozen.
For the caper butter, in a small mixing bowl mash the capers with a fork. Add the softened butter or margarine and fines herbes; stir till well combined.

Look for fines herbes in the spice section of the supermarket. It's a convenient mixture of thyme, oregano, sage, rosemary, marjoram, and basil.

1 tablespoon snipped parsley

● Grill salmon, on an uncovered grill, directly over *medium-hot* coals for 7 minutes. Turn and grill for 3 minutes. Brush salmon with *some* of the caper butter. Continue grilling for 3 to 5 minutes more or till salmon flakes easily when tested with a fork. Transfer to a serving platter. Brush with the remaining caper butter and sprinkle with parsley. Makes 4 servings.

Southern-Style Barbecue

No matter what part of the country you live in, your family and friends will enjoy this old-fashioned barbecue—done the Southern way! Have each guest family bring one of the following side dishes and you provide the meat. You'll need at least two grills—one for the Texas Barbecued Brisket and one for the Tennessee Ribs. (See pages 46 to 49 for recipes.)

MENU
Texas Barbecued Brisket
Tennessee Ribs
Saucy Beans
Creamy Potato Salad
Cabbage 'n' Spinach Slaw
Buttered French bread
Butter Pecan Ice Cream
Lemonade or iced tea

Texas Barbecued Brisket

Pictured on pages 44 and 45.

1½ to 2 pounds mesquite wood chunks	● At least one hour before grilling, soak wood chunks in enough water to cover.
¾ cup water ¼ cup Worcestershire sauce 2 tablespoons cider vinegar 2 tablespoons cooking oil 2 cloves garlic, minced ½ teaspoon instant beef bouillon granules ½ teaspoon dry mustard ½ teaspoon chili powder ¼ teaspoon ground red pepper	● For the brushing sauce, in a small mixing bowl combine water, Worcestershire sauce, cider vinegar, cooking oil, minced garlic, instant beef bouillon granules, dry mustard, chili powder, and ground red pepper. Set ½ *cup* of the brushing sauce aside for the serving sauce.
1 5- to 6-pound fresh beef brisket	● Drain wood chunks. In a covered grill arrange preheated coals around a drip pan; test for *slow* heat above pan. Place about *one-fourth* of the drained wood chunks on top of the preheated coals. Place brisket on grill rack, fat side up, over drip pan but not over coals. Brush with brushing sauce; lower grill hood. Grill for 2½ to 3 hours or till tender, brushing with the sauce every 30 minutes and adding more dampened wood chunks, if necessary.
½ cup catsup 2 tablespoons brown sugar 2 tablespoons butter *or* margarine Catsup	● Meanwhile, prepare the serving sauce. In a small saucepan combine the ½ cup reserved brushing sauce, the ½ cup catsup, brown sugar, and butter or margarine. On the range top, heat the mixture through and add additional catsup to achieve desired consistency. To serve, slice brisket across the grain and pass with the serving sauce. Makes 15 to 18 servings.

MENU COUNTDOWN
Host family—
4 hours ahead: Soak the mesquite chunks and hickory chips separately.
3½ hours ahead: Light charcoal in both grills. Prepare both brushing sauces.
3 hours ahead: Start grilling the Texas Barbecued Brisket.
2 hours ahead: Start grilling Tennessee Ribs on the second grill.
20 minutes ahead: Prepare both serving sauces.
Guest family 1—
3 hours ahead: Prepare Saucy Beans.
Guest family 2—
7 hours ahead: Prepare Creamy Potato Salad.
Guest family 3—
Several hours ahead: Prepare Cabbage 'n' Spinach Slaw.
Guest family 4—
Several hours ahead: Prepare Butter Pecan Ice Cream.
Guest family 5—
Prepare lemonade or iced tea and buttered French bread.

Tennessee Ribs

Pictured on pages 44 and 45.

8 cups hickory wood chips	● At least one hour before grilling, soak wood chips in enough water to cover.
⅓ cup finely chopped onion 2 tablespoons butter *or* margarine 2 teaspoons dry mustard 2 cups vegetable juice cocktail ⅔ cup vinegar ¼ cup molasses ½ teaspoon dried rosemary, crushed ½ teaspoon dried thyme, crushed ¼ teaspoon salt	● For brushing sauce, in a saucepan on the range top cook onion in butter or margarine till tender but not brown. Stir in the dry mustard. Add the vegetable juice cocktail, vinegar, molasses, rosemary, thyme, and salt. Bring mixture to boiling and reduce heat. Simmer, uncovered, for 5 minutes.
4 to 6 pounds pork country-style ribs (see tip, far right)	● Drain wood chips. In a covered grill arrange preheated coals around a drip pan; test for *slow* heat above pan. Sprinkle *one-fourth* (about 2 cups) of the drained chips over the preheated coals. Place ribs on grill rack over drip pan but not over coals. Brush ribs with sauce. Lower grill hood. Grill for 1½ to 2 hours or till no pink remains, brushing with the sauce and adding more dampened chips every 30 minutes.
	● About 15 minutes before serving, place the remaining brushing sauce on the range top. Bring to boiling; reduce heat. Simmer, uncovered, for 15 minutes or to achieve desired consistency. Pass sauce with ribs. Makes 6 to 8 servings.

Before the barbecue day, make sure your grill is large enough to handle the ribs. Most average-size grills can only hold about four pounds of ribs. So unless you have a *very* large grill, you'll need another grill or a rib rack.

Most rib racks can increase the cooking space up to 50 percent by letting you stand your rib pieces up rather than laying them flat down on the grill. Some rib racks are also designed to cook potatoes and/or ears of corn in an upright position.

Saucy Beans

Pictured on pages 44 and 45.

| 6 slices bacon, cut into 1-inch pieces
2 medium onions, chopped (1 cup)
1 medium green pepper, chopped (¾ cup)
4 21-ounce cans pork and beans in tomato sauce
½ cup packed brown sugar
½ cup catsup
¼ to ½ cup molasses
3 tablespoons Worcestershire sauce | ● In a skillet on the range top partially cook bacon. Drain, reserving 1 tablespoon fat; set bacon aside. In the skillet cook onion and green pepper in the reserved fat till tender but not brown.

In a large mixing bowl combine the cooked bacon, onion, green pepper, pork and beans, brown sugar, catsup, molasses, and Worcestershire sauce.

Pour mixture into a 4-quart casserole or Dutch oven. Bake, uncovered, in a 325° oven for 2½ hours, stirring occasionally. Makes 20 to 24 servings. |

This recipe has all the makings of the perfect potluck food—it's easy-to-fix and easy-to-tote. After you've baked the beans, transfer them to an electric slow crockery cooker to keep them warm.

Creamy Potato Salad

Pictured on pages 44 and 45.

14 medium potatoes (about 5 pounds)	● In a large covered saucepan on the range top, cook the potatoes in enough boiling water to cover for 20 to 25 minutes or till almost tender; drain. Peel and slice cooked potatoes.	**We didn't take any short-cuts with this potato salad—we made this mayonnaise dressing from scratch.**

1½ cups chopped celery
½ cup sliced green onion
⅓ cup sweet pickle relish
Cream Dressing (see recipe, far right)

● In a large mixing bowl combine the potatoes, celery, green onion, and pickle relish. Add the Cream Dressing; toss lightly with the potato mixture. Cover and chill at least 6 hours or overnight.

⅔ cup sliced radishes
Lettuce leaves (optional)
Hard-cooked egg slices (optional)

● Before serving, fold the radishes into the potato salad.

To serve, line bowl with lettuce leaves and garnish potato salad with hard-cooked egg slices, if desired. Makes 20 to 24 servings.

Cream Dressing: In a saucepan combine 1 tablespoon *sugar,* 1 tablespoon all-purpose *flour,* 2 teaspoons *salt,* 2 teaspoons *dry mustard,* and ¼ teaspoon *pepper.* Add 4 slightly beaten *egg yolks* and 1 cup *milk.* On the range top, cook and stir till thickened. Stir in ⅓ cup *vinegar* and ¼ cup *butter* or *margarine;* cool.

Whip 1 cup *whipping cream* till soft peaks form; fold into cooked mixture. Makes 3½ cups.

Cabbage 'n' Spinach Slaw

Pictured on pages 44 and 45.

¾ cup red wine vinegar
½ cup salad oil
⅓ cup sugar
1 teaspoon salt
½ teaspoon celery seed
½ teaspoon pepper
3 medium apples, cored and chopped
3 cups sliced fresh mushrooms

● In a mixing bowl combine vinegar, salad oil, sugar, salt, celery seed, and pepper; stir till sugar is dissolved.

Add chopped apple and sliced mushrooms; cover and chill mixture for several hours.

Add a new twist to an old favorite by making this unique coleslaw that includes chopped apple, spinach, and mushrooms.

1 small head red cabbage, shredded (5 cups)
1 small head green cabbage, shredded (5 cups)
4 ounces spinach, torn (3 cups)

● In a very large bowl combine red and green cabbage and spinach. Cover and chill till serving time.

To serve, combine the apple and cabbage mixtures; toss lightly. Makes 20 to 24 servings.

Butter Pecan Ice Cream

1 cup coarsely chopped pecans ½ cup sugar 2 tablespoons butter *or* margarine	● In a heavy 8-inch skillet combine pecans, sugar, and butter or margarine. On the range top heat mixture over medium heat, stirring constantly, for 6 to 8 minutes or till sugar melts and turns a rich brown color. Remove from heat and spread nuts on a buttered baking sheet or foil; separate into clusters. Cool. Break clusters into small chunks.
4 cups light cream 2 cups packed brown sugar 1 tablespoon vanilla	● In a large mixing bowl combine light cream, brown sugar, and vanilla; stir till sugar is dissolved.
4 cups whipping cream	● Stir in the pecan mixture and whipping cream.
Crushed ice Rock salt	● Pour the cream mixture into a 4- to 5-quart ice cream freezer container. Freeze cream mixture according to the manufacturer's directions, using crushed ice and rock salt. Makes about 3½ quarts or 24 servings.

To add a crunchy candy coating to the pecans, place the pecans, sugar, and butter in a heavy skillet. Heat and stir over medium heat till sugar melts and turns a rich brown color.

Caribbean Ribs

½ of a 6-ounce can (⅓ cup) frozen pineapple juice concentrate, thawed
¼ cup pineapple preserves
2 tablespoons rum
⅛ teaspoon salt
⅛ teaspoon ground cloves
⅛ teaspoon ground nutmeg

● For glaze, in a mixing bowl stir together the thawed pineapple juice concentrate, pineapple preserves, rum, salt, ground cloves, and ground nutmeg; set glaze aside.

Are you longing for a trip to the Caribbean islands? These ribs can help you vacation there—for one brief meal. Just take a bite, close your eyes, and let your imagination go!

4 pounds pork spareribs *or* pork loin back ribs

● In a covered grill arrange preheated coals around a drip pan; test for *medium* heat above the pan. Place ribs in a rib rack, if desired. Place ribs on grill rack over drip pan but not over coals. Lower grill hood. Grill for 1 hour.
　Brush glaze once onto ribs. Continue grilling, in a covered grill, for 15 to 20 minutes more or till no pink remains.
　Just before serving, brush ribs with the glaze again. Makes 4 to 6 servings.

Apricot-Glazed Ham

1 16-ounce can unpeeled apricot halves
¼ cup packed brown sugar
4 teaspoons vinegar
2 teaspoons prepared mustard
½ teaspoon ground cinnamon

● For glaze, drain apricots, reserving ¼ cup syrup. Set six apricot halves aside for garnish. In a blender container or food processor bowl place the remaining apricot halves; cover and blend till smooth. Add the reserved syrup, brown sugar, vinegar, mustard, and cinnamon; cover and blend till well combined.

For glistening results without danger of burning, brush the glaze on near the end of grilling.

1 5- to 7-pound fully cooked boneless ham
Whole cloves

● Score ham by making shallow cuts diagonally across the surface in a diamond pattern. Stud with cloves. Insert a meat thermometer near center of ham.

● In a covered grill arrange preheated coals around a drip pan; test for *medium* heat above pan. Place ham on rack over pan but not over coals. Lower hood. Grill for 1¼ hours. Brush ham with glaze. Grill about 15 minutes more or till meat thermometer registers 140°.

Watercress

● Heat the remaining glaze on the side of the grill to pass with ham.
　Just before serving, brush ham with glaze again; garnish with reserved apricot halves and watercress. Serves 12 to 16.

After scoring the ham, stud it with cloves by pressing the stem portions of the cloves into the ham.

Cranberry Leg of Lamb

1 8-ounce can whole
   cranberry sauce
⅔ cup rosé wine
2 tablespoons snipped
   chives
2 tablespoons honey
2 tablespoons cooking oil
1 tablespoon tarragon
   vinegar
2 teaspoons cornstarch
⅛ teaspoon salt

● For the cranberry glaze, in a saucepan combine whole cranberry sauce, rosé wine, snipped chives, honey, cooking oil, tarragon vinegar, cornstarch, and salt. On the range top, cook and stir mixture till thickened and bubbly. Cook and stir for 2 minutes more. Remove glaze from heat and set aside.

With a little bit of ingenuity, we've made grilling a leg of lamb as easy as grilling a steak. Have your butcher bone the leg of lamb and slit it lengthwise. Then use either long skewers or a wire grill basket to keep the meat flat during grilling.

1 5- to 6-pound leg of lamb,
   boned and butterflied

● Spread the leg of lamb out flat like a thick steak. Trim any excess fat and fell (a thin membrane covering the meat and fat) from meat. Insert two long skewers through meat at right angles, making a cross, *or* place meat in a wire grill basket.

● Grill lamb, on an uncovered grill, directly over *medium* coals to desired doneness, allowing about 1 hour for medium and turning *every* 15 minutes. Brush often with the cranberry glaze during the last 20 minutes of grilling.
   Heat any of the remaining glaze on the side of the grill.

● Transfer lamb to a cutting board; remove skewers, if used. Let stand for 15 minutes. To serve, slice the meat thinly across the grain and pass with the remaining glaze. Makes 8 to 10 servings.

Citrus-Glazed Lamb Chops

½ cup orange marmalade
2 tablespoons lemon juice
1 teaspoon dried mint, crushed

6 lamb loin chops, cut 1 inch thick

● For the glaze, in a small saucepan combine the orange marmalade, lemon juice, and mint. On the range top, cook and stir till heated through.

● Grill lamb chops, on an uncovered grill, directly over *medium* coals for 10 minutes. Turn and grill to desired doneness, allowing 10 to 15 minutes more for medium. Brush often with glaze during the last 5 minutes of grilling.
    Just before serving, brush lamb chops with glaze again. Makes 6 servings.

Keep the chops juicy by handling them with tongs, rather than piercing them with a fork.

Speed Up Cleanup

Cleaning up the grill doesn't have to be a dirty chore. Here are a few suggestions to help make it easier, faster, and less messy.
● Before building the fire, line the inside of the firebox with *heavy* foil. Then, after you've finished grilling and the ashes are cold, just pick up the foil and throw it away.
● Clean the grill rack right after cooking. (Read the cleaning and care directions supplied with your equipment before using any cleaning products or abrasives.) Or, you can take a preventive step and spray the cold grill rack with a nonstick vegetable spray coating before cooking.
    To clean the grill rack, remove the rack from over the coals. Cover both sides of the rack with wet paper towels or newspapers and let stand while you eat. Later, the burned-on food will usually wash off. To remove stubborn burned-on food, sprinkle dry baking soda on a damp sponge and scour lightly. Or, use a scouring or abrasive-type pad, crumpled foil, or a stiff grill brush.
● Clean the inside of your gas grill by turning the gas burners to HIGH. Close the hood and let the grill burn about 15 minutes. Let the grill cool and remove the burned food particles from the grill rack. Once a year, remove the grill rack, briquettes, and briquette rack, and brush out the bottom of your grill.

Honey-Glazed Chicken

¼ cup honey
3 tablespoons prepared mustard
2 tablespoons butter *or* margarine
1 tablespoon Worcestershire sauce

● For glaze, in a small saucepan combine the honey, prepared mustard, butter or margarine, and Worcestershire sauce. On the range top, heat and stir the mixture till butter or margarine melts.

Can't wait to sink your teeth into the succulent flavors of this barbecued chicken? You can save time by micro-cooking the chicken while the coals are preheating.

6 chicken legs (about 4 pounds)

● Cut the drumsticks from thighs.
Grill chicken pieces, on an uncovered grill, directly over *medium* coals for 20 minutes. Turn and grill for 10 to 20 minutes more or till tender, brushing often with the glaze during the last 10 minutes of grilling.
Just before serving, brush chicken with the glaze again. Makes 6 servings.

● **Microwave method:** Arrange *half* of the drumsticks and thighs in a shallow, nonmetal baking dish, as shown at right. Cover dish loosely with clear plastic wrap or waxed paper.
Place in a countertop microwave oven and cook chicken on 100% power (HIGH) about 8 minutes or till chicken is nearly tender, giving the dish a half-turn once during cooking. Repeat with the remaining drumsticks and thighs.
Transfer the micro-cooked chicken to the grill rack. Grill chicken pieces, on an uncovered grill, directly over *medium* coals for 5 minutes. Turn and grill for 5 to 7 minutes more or till tender, brushing often with the glaze during the last 5 minutes of grilling.

To help ensure even cooking in the microwave oven, arrange the chicken pieces in a shallow, nonmetal baking dish, with the meatiest portions toward the outside.

Chicken with Peach Glaze

1 **8-ounce can peach slices, drained**
2 **tablespoons teriyaki sauce**
2 **tablespoons honey**
1 **tablespoon cooking oil**
1 **teaspoon grated gingerroot**
1 **teaspoon sesame seed**

● Reserve 2 or 3 peach slices for garnish, if desired. For glaze, in a blender container or food processor bowl combine the remaining peaches, teriyaki sauce, honey, cooking oil, and grated gingerroot; cover and blend till mixture is smooth. Stir in the sesame seed.

1 **2½- to 3-pound broiler-fryer chicken**
  Salt

● Rinse chicken; pat excess moisture from the chicken with paper towels. Sprinkle the inside of the cavities with salt. Skewer the neck skin to the back of the chicken. Tie legs to tail with cord. Twist wing tips under back.

● In a covered grill arrange the preheated coals around a drip pan; test for *medium* heat above the pan. Place the chicken, breast side up, on the grill rack over the drip pan but not over coals. Lower grill hood. Grill for 55 minutes. Brush chicken once with the glaze and continue grilling, in a covered grill, for 5 to 10 minutes more or till a drumstick moves easily in its socket.

Heat the remaining glaze on the side of the grill to pass with the chicken. Garnish chicken with the reserved peach slices, if desired. Makes 6 servings.

● **Rotisserie method:** Skewer neck skin to back of chicken. Insert spit rod lengthwise through chicken. Tie a piece of cord around chicken to prevent legs and wings from flopping. Adjust holding forks and test balance. Attach spit to highest setting on grill; turn motor on. Grill chicken, on an uncovered grill, directly over *medium* coals for 1¼ to 1½ hours or till drumstick moves easily in its socket. Brush with the glaze during the last 5 to 10 minutes of grilling. Heat remaining glaze and garnish as above.

Adding a colorful garnish can make the difference between an everyday meal and a festive occasion. Reserve a few of the peach slices while making the glaze and use them along with some watercress or curly endive to garnish the chicken.

Cinnamon-Beef Kabobs

1 pound boneless beef eye round steak, cut into ¾-inch cubes
12 large whole fresh mushrooms
⅓ cup cooking oil
⅓ cup dry red wine
1 clove garlic, minced
4 inches stick cinnamon, broken, *or* ½ teaspoon ground cinnamon
4 whole cloves *or* ⅛ teaspoon ground cloves
1 teaspoon dried basil, crushed
¼ teaspoon salt
8 boiling onions
2 large tomatoes, cut into 8 wedges

● Place the meat cubes and mushrooms in a plastic bag; set in a bowl.

For the marinade, in a mixing bowl combine the oil, wine, garlic, cinnamon, cloves, basil, and salt; pour over the meat and mushrooms in the bag. Close bag.

Marinate the meat and mushrooms in the refrigerator for 6 hours or overnight, turning the bag several times.

In a saucepan on the range top precook onions in a small amount of boiling water for 4 minutes; drain.

Drain the meat and mushrooms, reserving the marinade.

On four skewers alternately thread the meat, mushrooms, onions, and tomato wedges. Place on a kabob rack, if desired.

● Grill kabobs, on an uncovered grill, over *medium-hot* coals to desired doneness, allowing 6 to 8 minutes for medium. Turn and brush often with the reserved marinade during grilling. Makes 4 servings.

One taste panel member remarked, "Cinnamon adds an unexpected, interesting flavor to these kabobs." Serve the *Cinnamon-Beef Kabobs* over cooked bulgur or wheat berries and top with yogurt.

Leek and Beef Kabobs

2 large carrots, cut into 1-inch-thick slices
2 large leeks, cut into 1-inch pieces
⅓ cup pineapple preserves
⅓ cup catsup
2 tablespoons red wine vinegar
1 tablespoon brown sugar
1 tablespoon lemon juice
1 tablespoon cooking oil

● In a saucepan on the range top precook carrots in a small amount of boiling water for 11 minutes. Add leeks and continue cooking for 4 minutes more; drain and set vegetables aside.

For glaze, in a small saucepan combine pineapple preserves, catsup, red wine vinegar, brown sugar, lemon juice, and cooking oil. On the range top, cook mixture, uncovered, for 10 minutes, stirring occasionally.

1 pound boneless beef sirloin steak, cut into 1-inch cubes

● On four skewers alternately thread carrots, leek pieces, and meat. Place on a kabob rack, if desired.

Grill, on an uncovered grill, over *medium-hot* coals to desired doneness, allowing 9 to 11 minutes for medium. Turn often during grilling; brush with glaze during the last 2 minutes of grilling. Makes 4 servings.

The trick to getting the meat and vegetables done at the same time when grilling kabobs is to leave a little space between each piece when threading them onto a skewer. This way the pieces will cook evenly.

Zucchini-Beef Kabobs

1 **pound beef round** *or* **chuck steak, cut into 1-inch cubes** ⅔ **cup tomato sauce** ½ **cup sake** *or* **dry white wine** 1 **small onion, finely chopped** 1 **clove garlic, minced** 2 **tablespoons vinegar** 1 **tablespoon brown sugar** ½ **teaspoon paprika** ¼ **teaspoon dried marjoram, crushed** 1 **teaspoon Worcestershire sauce** ¼ **teaspoon salt**	● Place the meat cubes in a plastic bag; set in a bowl. For marinade, in a mixing bowl combine tomato sauce, sake or dry white wine, finely chopped onion, minced garlic, vinegar, brown sugar, paprika, marjoram, Worcestershire sauce, and salt; pour marinade over meat in the bag. Close the bag. Marinate the meat in the refrigerator for 6 hours or overnight, turning bag several times.	**When you're on the go, kabobs are a great make-ahead meal. Marinate the meat and precook the vegetables ahead of time. Complete your meal with rice. You can cook the rice at the same time you're precooking the vegetables. Then refrigerate the rice until you're ready to use it. To reheat, in a saucepan add about 2 tablespoons water for each cup of cooked rice. Then cover and simmer till hot.**
12 **large whole fresh mushrooms** 3 **small zucchini, cut into 1-inch-thick slices**	● In a saucepan on the range top precook the mushrooms and zucchini slices in a small amount of boiling water for 1 to 2 minutes or till slightly tender; drain vegetables. Drain meat, reserving marinade.	
	● On four skewers alternately thread the mushrooms, zucchini slices, and meat. Place on a kabob rack, if desired. Grill kabobs, on an uncovered grill, directly over *medium-hot* coals to desired doneness, allowing 9 to 11 minutes for medium. Turn and brush often with the reserved marinade during grilling.	
	● Heat any of the remaining marinade on the side of the grill to pass with the kabobs. Makes 4 servings.	

Make-Your-Own Kabobs

Have a create-your-own-kabob contest! Let your guests pick and choose ingredients from each of the columns. Allow about ⅓ pound of shrimp, meat, or poultry for each guest. After everyone has made their kabob, share in the fun of judging the best-tasting or most imaginative kabob.

- Thaw the shrimp, if frozen. Shell and devein shrimp.
- Precook vegetables, if necessary.
- Prepare sauces as directed.
- Arrange shrimp, meat, poultry, and vegetables on a platter or in individual containers. Cover; chill till serving time.
- On skewers alternately thread any combination of meat and vegetables. Place the full skewers on a kabob rack, if desired.
- Grill kabobs, on an uncovered grill, directly over *hot* coals for 8 to 12 minutes or to desired doneness. Turn and brush often with the desired sauce.

*Note: In a saucepan on the range top precook these vegetables separately in a small amount of boiling water for 1 to 2 minutes (4 minutes for the boiling onions). Drain; cover and chill vegetables till grilling time.

CHICKEN

BEEF

+ **Meat**	+ **Vegetables**	+ **Sauce**
Fresh *or* frozen jumbo shrimp in shells	Cherry tomatoes	Sesame Curry Sauce
Cooked brat- wurst, cut into 2-inch pieces	Peeled jicama, cut into 1-inch pieces	Onion-Mustard Sauce
Chicken, lamb, *or* beef, cut into 1½-inch cubes	Small whole fresh mush- rooms*	Dilly Butter- Garlic Sauce
	Sweet red *or* green pepper, cut into 1-inch squares*	1½ cups bottled hickory smoke- flavored barbe- cue sauce
	Zucchini, cut into 1-inch-thick slices*	
	Yellow summer squash, cut into 1-inch cubes*	
	Boiling onions*	

SHRIMP

Sesame Curry Sauce: In a screw-top jar combine ½ cup *soy sauce*, ⅓ cup *cooking oil*, ¼ cup *honey*, ¼ cup *vinegar*, 1 tablespoon toasted *sesame seed*, 1 teaspoon *curry powder*, and ¼ teaspoon *pepper*. Cover and shake well. Makes about 1½ cups.

Onion-Mustard Sauce: In a small bowl combine ½ cup *Dijon-style mustard*, ⅓ cup *catsup*, 3 tablespoons *mayonnaise* or *salad dressing*, 2 tablespoons finely chopped *green onion*, and 1 tablespoon *water*. Cover and chill for several hours to blend flavors. Makes about 1 cup.

Dilly Butter-Garlic Sauce: In a saucepan on the range top melt 2 tablespoons *butter* or *margarine*. Add 2 small cloves minced *garlic;* cook for 1 minute. Add an additional ¾ cup *butter* or *margarine* to pan and 1½ teaspoons snipped *fresh dill* or ½ teaspoon *dried dillweed*. Heat till butter or margarine is melted. Stir in 3 tablespoons *lemon juice*. Makes about 1 cup.

Skewered Lamb

2	**pounds boneless lamb, cut into 1-inch cubes**
½	**cup burgundy**
⅓	**cup olive oil *or* cooking oil**
1	**teaspoon salt**
1	**teaspoon dried mint, crushed**
¾	**teaspoon dried thyme, crushed**
¾	**teaspoon dried basil, crushed**

● Place lamb cubes in a plastic bag; set in a bowl.

For the marinade, in a mixing bowl combine burgundy, olive oil or cooking oil, salt, mint, thyme, and basil; pour over lamb in the bag. Close the bag. Marinate lamb in refrigerator for 6 hours or overnight, turning bag several times.

Threading crisp vegetables onto a skewer can sometimes be tricky because the vegetables may tend to break. To eliminate this problem, our Test Kitchen recommends precooking the vegetables until they're slightly tender.

1¼	**pounds boiling onions**
2	**medium green peppers, cut into 1-inch squares**

● In a saucepan on the range top precook onions in a small amount of boiling water for 3 minutes. Add green pepper and continue cooking for 1 to 2 minutes more or till vegetables are slightly tender; drain vegetables.

Drain lamb, reserving marinade.

8	***or* 16 cherry tomatoes**

● On eight long skewers or 16 short skewers, alternately thread onions, green pepper, and lamb. Place on kabob rack, if desired.

Grill kabobs, on an uncovered grill, directly over *hot* coals to desired doneness, allowing 10 to 12 minutes for medium. Turn and brush with reserved marinade several times during grilling.

Garnish each skewer with a tomato. Makes 8 servings.

Turn Your Kabobs with Ease

Do your kabobs stick or fall apart when you try to turn them? If so, consider using a skewer and holder set. It can be used on any type of grill and is available wherever other barbecuing accessories are sold.

The skewer and holder set consists of four to six long skewers and a rack. The rack holds the full skewers slightly above the grill rack, allowing the kabobs to be picked up and rotated more easily. You also can use the set to serve the finished kabobs by transferring it to a platter.

Sausage Sampler Kabobs

4 slices bacon, diced
¾ cup chopped onion
2 tablespoons all-purpose flour
4 teaspoons sugar
⅛ teaspoon pepper
¾ cup beer
⅓ cup water
¼ cup vinegar
   Few drops Kitchen Bouquet (optional)

● For sauce, in a skillet on the range top partially cook the bacon; add onion and cook till onion is tender but not brown. Stir in flour, sugar, and pepper. Add beer, water, and vinegar. Cook and stir onion mixture till thickened and bubbly. Cook and stir the mixture for 1 minute more. Stir in a few drops of Kitchen Bouquet, if desired.

12 small new potatoes (about 1¾ pounds)
1 green pepper, cut into 1-inch squares

● Peel a strip from the middle of each potato. In a saucepan on the range top cook the potatoes, covered, in enough boiling water to cover for 8 minutes.
   Add green pepper and continue cooking vegetables, covered, for 1 to 2 minutes more or till green pepper is slightly tender; drain and set the vegetables aside.

5 bratwurst links (about 16 ounces)
3 mild Italian sausage links (about 10 ounces)
3 Polish sausage links (about 8 ounces)

● Place bratwurst, Italian, and Polish sausage links in a large saucepan. Add enough water to cover. On the range top, bring to boiling and reduce heat. Simmer, covered, for 10 to 12 minutes or till done; drain. Cut the sausages crosswise into 2- to 2½-inch pieces.

● On six 10- to 12-inch skewers alternately thread potatoes, green pepper pieces, and sausage pieces. Place on a kabob rack, if desired.
   Grill, on an uncovered grill, directly over *hot* coals for 10 to 12 minutes or till heated through, turning and brushing often with the sauce during grilling.
   Heat any of the remaining sauce on the side of the grill to pass with kabobs. Makes 6 servings.

Now's your chance to not only sample different sausages on your kabobs, but also to taste-test some different vegetables.
   Try substituting 1-inch pieces of corn on the cob, onion wedges, and/or baby carrots for the new potatoes. Precook these vegetables in a small amount of boiling water for 1 to 2 minutes or till slightly tender before threading them onto skewers.

Sweet 'n' Sour Chicken Kabobs

1 cup fresh *or* frozen brussels sprouts
3 medium carrots, cut into 1½-inch-thick slices

● Cut any of the large fresh brussels sprouts in half.

In a saucepan on the range top precook carrots in a small amount of boiling water for 15 minutes. Add brussels sprouts; bring water back to boiling. Continue cooking vegetables for 5 minutes more or till slightly tender; drain and set vegetables aside.

2 whole medium chicken breasts, skinned, halved lengthwise, boned, and cut into 2x½-inch strips

● Wrap *one* chicken strip around *one* brussels sprout and *one* carrot slice. On four 12-inch skewers thread the chicken-wrapped brussels sprouts and carrot slices.

Place the kabobs in a 13x9x2-inch baking dish.

⅓ cup Italian salad dressing
1 8¼-ounce can crushed pineapple
½ cup hot-style catsup
1 tablespoon soy sauce
½ teaspoon lemon pepper

● For marinade, in a medium mixing bowl combine salad dressing, *undrained* pineapple, catsup, soy sauce, and lemon pepper; pour over kabobs in the dish. Turn kabobs to coat with the marinade. Cover and marinate kabobs in the refrigerator for 6 hours or overnight, turning the kabobs several times.

● Drain kabobs, reserving marinade. Place on a kabob rack, if desired.

Grill kabobs, on an uncovered grill, directly over *medium-hot* coals for 10 to 12 minutes or till chicken and vegetables are tender, turning and brushing often with the reserved marinade.

● For sauce, in a small saucepan on the range top bring the remaining marinade to boiling; reduce heat. Simmer, uncovered, for 10 minutes or to achieve desired consistency. Pass sauce with kabobs. Makes 4 servings.

For anyone who hates cleanup, this tip is for you. Along with using paper plates and cups, also use disposable bamboo skewers. To prevent the bamboo skewers from burning, soak them in water for 30 minutes.

Curried Shrimp Kabobs

1 large clove garlic, minced
½ teaspoon finely shredded
   lime peel (set aside)
2 tablespoons lime juice
2 teaspoons curry powder
¼ cup cooking oil
⅛ teaspoon salt
   Dash onion powder

● For sauce, in a small saucepan on the range top cook garlic, lime juice, and curry powder in cooking oil for 1 minute. Stir in shredded lime peel, salt, and onion powder.

The tricky part about making these kabobs is wrapping the pea pods around the shrimp. As you thread the shrimp onto the skewer, wrap one pea pod around half of the shrimp and a second pea pod around the other half.

---

1 pound fresh *or* frozen
   jumbo shrimp in shells
½ of a 6-ounce package
   frozen pea pods, thawed
1 papaya, peeled, halved,
   seeded, and cut into 1-
   to 1½-inch pieces

● Thaw shrimp, if frozen. Shell and devein shrimp; set aside.

   Wrap *two* pea pods around *each* shrimp. On four 9-inch skewers alternately thread shrimp and papaya. Place on a kabob rack, if desired. Brush kabobs with sauce.

   Grill, on an uncovered grill, over *medium-hot* coals for 10 to 12 minutes or till shrimp is pink, turning often. Brush kabobs with sauce; serve. Serves 4.

Shrimp-Stuffed Roast

½ cup chopped celery
¼ cup snipped chives
2 tablespoons butter *or* margarine
12 ounces shelled shrimp, cooked and chopped
½ cup plain croutons
¼ cup dry white wine
¾ teaspoon finely shredded lemon peel
⅛ teaspoon salt
⅛ teaspoon cracked pepper

● For the stuffing, in a skillet on the range top cook the celery and chives in butter or margarine till celery is tender but not brown. Stir in the chopped shrimp, plain croutons, dry white wine, finely shredded lemon peel, salt, and cracked pepper.

This beef roast is utterly delicious. An excellent choice when entertaining, it's not only easy but it's also very elegant.

1 5-pound boneless beef rib roast, rolled and tied

● Untie and unroll roast; spread stuffing evenly over roast. Reroll roast and stuffing together; tie together securely with cord.

● Insert a meat thermometer near center of roast. In a covered grill arrange preheated coals around a drip pan; test for *medium* heat above pan. Place roast on grill rack over drip pan but not over coals. Lower grill hood. Grill till meat thermometer registers 140° for rare (about 2½ hours), 160° for medium (about 3 hours), and 170° for well-done (about 3¼ hours). Transfer roast to a cutting board; let stand for 15 minutes before slicing. Makes 12 to 15 servings.

Adjusting the Heat

Some recipes require hot coals for cooking, and others require slow coals. If you haven't got exactly the fire you need (see page 7), adjust the temperature of the coals by following these suggestions:
● When coals are too hot, either raise the grill rack, spread the coals apart, close the air vents halfway, or remove some of the hot briquettes. In a gas or electric grill, adjust the burner to a lower setting.
● Increase the temperature of your coals by tapping the ashes off the burning coals with tongs, moving the coals closer together, adding more briquettes, lowering the grill rack, or opening the vents to allow more air to circulate through the grill. In a gas or electric grill, adjust the burner to a higher setting.

Steak and Spinach Tournedos

1 1- to 1½-pound beef flank steak ¼ teaspoon salt Dash pepper	● Using the coarse-tooth side of a meat mallet, pound the flank steak into a 12x8-inch rectangle, working from the center out to edges. Score one side of steak, using a sharp knife to make shallow cuts diagonally across steak in a diamond pattern. Sprinkle with salt and pepper; set steak aside.
1 beaten egg 1 10-ounce package frozen chopped spinach, cooked and well drained ⅓ cup fine dry bread crumbs	● For filling, in a mixing bowl combine egg and cooked spinach. Stir in dry bread crumbs. Spread filling over unscored side of steak. Starting from narrow end, roll up steak, jelly-roll style. Skewer with wooden toothpicks at 1-inch intervals. Cut the roll between the toothpicks into eight 1-inch slices. Secure with decorative skewers, if desired.
	● Grill steaks, on an uncovered grill, directly over *medium* coals for 8 minutes. Turn and grill to desired doneness, allowing 8 to 10 minutes more for medium.
1 tablespoon butter *or* margarine 1 tablespoon all-purpose flour 2 tablespoons Dijon-style mustard 1 tablespoon prepared horseradish ½ cup milk ½ cup beef broth 1 tablespoon snipped chives 1 teaspoon lemon juice	● Meanwhile, for sauce, in a small saucepan on the range top melt butter or margarine. Stir in all-purpose flour, Dijon-style mustard, and prepared horseradish. Add milk and beef broth. Cook and stir till thickened and bubbly. Cook and stir for 1 minute more. Remove from heat; stir in snipped chives and lemon juice.
	● To serve, remove toothpicks or skewers from meat rolls; pass with the warm sauce. Makes 4 servings.

For a colorful side dish, serve *Vegetable Kabobs* (see recipe, page 91) with these *Steak and Spinach Tournedos.*

Using the fine-tooth side of a meat mallet, pound each piece of veal to ⅛-inch thickness, working from the center to the edges.

Sprinkle each piece of veal with about ⅓ cup of the cheese filling.

Fruit- and Cheese-Stuffed Veal Rolls

1 to 1¼ pounds boneless veal leg round steak, cut ¼ to ½ inch thick Salt Pepper	● Cut veal into four pieces; pound each piece with a meat mallet to ⅛-inch thickness. Sprinkle each piece with salt and pepper.
1 cup shredded Havarti *or* Swiss cheese ½ cup finely chopped apple *or* pear 2 tablespoons finely chopped pecans *or* walnuts 2 tablespoons snipped parsley	● For filling, in a small mixing bowl toss together the 1 cup shredded Havarti or Swiss cheese, the ½ cup chopped apple or pear, nuts, and parsley. Sprinkle about *⅓ cup* of filling atop each piece of veal. Fold in sides of veal; roll up jelly-roll style, gently pressing all edges together to seal. Secure veal rolls together with small metal skewers.
2 tablespoons butter *or* margarine, melted ¼ teaspoon ground nutmeg	● In a dish combine the melted butter or margarine and nutmeg. Brush veal rolls with *some* of the butter mixture. In a covered grill arrange preheated coals around a drip pan; test for *medium* heat above pan. Place veal rolls on grill rack over drip pan but not over coals. Lower hood. Grill to desired doneness, allowing 20 to 25 minutes for medium.
4 slices Havarti *or* Swiss cheese, cut into strips Apple *or* pear slices	● Brush veal rolls with the remaining butter mixture; remove skewers. To serve, top each veal roll with strips of Havarti or Swiss cheese; serve with apple or pear slices. Makes 4 servings.

The flavor of Havarti depends on its age. Buy the type of Havarti cheese that best suits your taste. This cream-color cheese will have a mild flavor with a slight aftertaste. With two or three months of aging, the flavor becomes more pungent.

Fold in the sides of each piece of veal. Roll up jelly-roll style, making sure the folded sides are included in the roll. Press all edges together gently to seal, and secure with small metal skewers.

Sensational Chops

¼ **cup maple-flavored syrup**
¼ **cup catsup**
2 **tablespoons dry white wine**
½ **teaspoon dry mustard**
   Dash ground ginger

● For sauce, in a small saucepan combine maple-flavored syrup, catsup, dry white wine, dry mustard, and ginger. On the range top, bring to boiling; remove from heat and set sauce aside.

Pork chops + apricot-rice filling + maple-flavored sauce adds up to sensational!

½ **cup water**
¼ **cup long grain rice**
3 **tablespoons snipped dried apricots**
1 **teaspoon instant chicken bouillon granules**
   Dash pepper

● For stuffing, in a saucepan combine water, rice, apricots, instant chicken bouillon granules, and pepper. Cover with a tight-fitting lid.
   On the range top, bring to boiling; reduce heat. Cook, covered, for 15 minutes. Remove from heat. Let stand, covered, for 10 minutes.

4 **pork loin rib chops, cut 1½ inches thick**
2 **tablespoons sliced green onion**

● Cut a pocket in *each* of the chops by cutting from fat side almost to bone.
   Stir onion into filling.
   Spoon about *¼ cup* of the filling into *each* pocket. Fasten pocket opening with wooden toothpicks, if necessary.

● Grill pork chops, in a covered grill, directly over *medium* coals for 20 minutes. Turn and grill for 20 to 25 minutes more or till no pink remains, brushing often with the sauce during the last 10 minutes of grilling.

● Heat any remaining sauce on the side of the grill. Just before serving, pour the remaining heated sauce over the chops. Makes 4 servings.

Chicken with Pecan-Rice Stuffing

Make stuffing easier by placing the bird, neck side down, in a mixing bowl. Lightly spoon the rice mixture into the body cavity of the bird.

¾ cup chopped onion
¾ cup chopped celery
¼ cup snipped parsley
¼ cup butter *or* margarine
2 cups cooked rice
½ cup chopped pecans
½ teaspoon salt
¼ teaspoon dried marjoram, crushed
¼ teaspoon dried thyme, crushed
¼ teaspoon pepper

● For stuffing, in a medium saucepan on the range top cook the chopped onion, chopped celery, and snipped parsley in butter or margarine till onion and celery are tender but not brown.

Remove from heat. Stir in the cooked rice, chopped pecans, the ½ teaspoon salt, marjoram, thyme, and pepper.

1 4- to 5-pound whole roasting chicken *or* one 6- to 7-pound capon
Salt

● Rinse the roasting chicken or capon; pat excess moisture from the bird with paper towels. Sprinkle inside of cavities with the additional salt.

Spoon some of the stuffing mixture into the neck cavity. Skewer neck skin to back of bird. Lightly spoon the stuffing into body cavity; do not pack. Tie legs to tail with cord and twist wing tips under back, as shown at right.

To close the body cavity, wrap a piece of cord around the tail and two legs. Then pull the cord together and tie securely.

● Place any remaining stuffing in center of a piece of *heavy* foil; bring up long edges of foil and, leaving a little space for expansion of steam, seal tightly with a double fold. Then fold short ends to seal.

Cooking oil

● In a covered grill arrange preheated coals around a drip pan; test for *medium* heat above pan. Place the stuffed bird, breast side up, on the grill rack over the drip pan but not over coals. Brush bird with cooking oil. Insert meat thermometer in the center of the inside thigh muscle, not touching bone. Lower grill hood. Grill for 1¼ to 1½ hours (about 2 hours for capon) or till meat thermometer registers 185°, brushing bird with oil every 30 minutes.

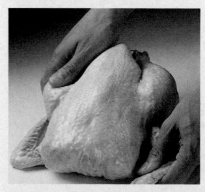

To make the bird more compact during grilling, place the bird on its back. Twist the tips of the wings under the back of the bird.

● Place foil packet of stuffing on grill rack with bird during the last 25 to 30 minutes of grilling to heat through. Makes 6 to 8 servings.

Little Stuffed Hens

½ cup chopped celery
½ cup thinly sliced green onion
¼ cup butter *or* margarine
1 8¼-ounce can crushed pineapple, drained
¼ cup chopped peanuts
3 tablespoons dry sherry
¼ teaspoon salt
¼ teaspoon dried thyme, crushed
1 8-ounce package (2 cups) cornbread stuffing mix

● For stuffing, in a skillet on the range top cook the chopped celery and thinly sliced green onion in butter or margarine till tender but not brown. Remove from heat and stir in the drained pineapple, chopped peanuts, dry sherry, the ¼ teaspoon salt, and thyme.

In a mixing bowl toss the pineapple mixture lightly with the stuffing mix.

Depending on the size of your grill, you can grill four to six Cornish game hens. When grilling less than six hens, warm the remaining stuffing in a foil packet on the grill for 20 to 25 minutes.

---

4 to 6 1- to 1¼-pound Cornish game hens
Salt

● Rinse hens; pat excess moisture from birds with paper towels. Sprinkle cavities with the additional salt; skewer neck skin to back of bird. Lightly spoon about ⅔ *cup* of the stuffing mixture into the body cavity of *each* bird; do not pack. Cover opening with foil. Tie the legs to tail with cord. Twist wing tips under back.

● Place any remaining stuffing in the center of a piece of *heavy* foil; bring up the long edges of foil and, leaving a little space for expansion of steam, seal tightly with a double fold. Then fold the short ends to seal.

¼ cup butter *or* margarine, melted

● In a covered grill arrange preheated coals around a drip pan; test for *medium* heat above the pan. Place the stuffed birds, breast side up and with space between birds, on the grill rack over the drip pan but not over coals. Brush the birds with melted butter or margarine. Lower grill hood. Grill for 1 to 1¼ hours or till tender.

● Place the foil packet of stuffing on the grill rack with the birds during the last 20 to 25 minutes of grilling to heat through. Makes 8 to 12 servings.

Bulgur-Stuffed Salmon Steaks

4 fresh *or* frozen salmon steaks, cut 1 inch thick (about 2 pounds) 2 cups hickory wood chips ½ cup bulgur wheat	● Thaw salmon, if frozen. 　At least one hour before grilling, soak hickory chips in enough water to cover. 　In a small mixing bowl cover bulgur with 1 inch of *boiling* water. Let bulgur stand 30 minutes; drain well.	**Complement the flavor of salmon by combining bulgur, lemon juice, and herbs for a nutty-tasting stuffing.**
2 tablespoons snipped parsley 1 tablespoon sliced green onion 1½ teaspoons snipped fresh coriander *or* ½ teaspoon ground coriander ¼ teaspoon salt	● For the stuffing, in the mixing bowl combine the drained bulgur, snipped parsley, sliced green onion, coriander, and salt; set the stuffing aside.	
Cooking oil 2 tablespoons lemon juice 2 tablespoons butter *or* margarine, melted	● Make a 12x8-inch pan with *heavy* foil (*see* illustration on page 22); lightly brush pan with cooking oil. Place salmon steaks in a single layer in the pan. 　In a small mixing bowl combine lemon juice and melted butter or margarine; brush onto salmon steaks. 　Spoon *one-fourth* of the stuffing mixture into the center cavity of *each* steak.	
	● Drain the hickory chips. In a covered grill arrange the preheated coals around the edge of the grill; test for *medium-hot* coals. Sprinkle the drained chips over the preheated coals. Place the foil pan containing salmon steaks on the center of the grill rack but not over coals. Lower grill hood. Grill for 25 minutes.	
Brown sugar (optional)	● Sprinkle steaks with *2 tablespoons* of brown sugar, if desired. Continue grilling, in a covered grill, for 5 minutes more or till the salmon flakes easily when tested with a fork. Before serving, sprinkle the grilled salmon steaks with additional brown sugar, if desired. Serves 4.	

Fancy Barbecue Menu

Grilling doesn't have to mean a backyard picnic. Using the wonderful flavors of barbecuing, you can create a truly elegant meal. This show-stopping dinner serves six to eight people. Prepare everything ahead of time. When your guests arrive, just take the meat from the grill, pour the wine, and enjoy! (See recipes on pages 74 and 75.)

MENU
Turkey-Ham Roll
Cauliflower 'n' Tomato Toss
Breadsticks
White wine
Water with lemon
Raspberry Chantilly
Coffee

Turkey-Ham Roll

Pictured on pages 72 and 73.

1 2-pound fresh *or* frozen turkey half breast with skin	● Thaw turkey, if frozen. Remove and discard bones from turkey half breast, leaving skin attached. Place turkey half breast, skin side down, between two pieces of clear plastic wrap. Using the flat side of a meat mallet, pound the turkey breast into a 12x6-inch rectangle, working from the center to edges.
1 tablespoon lemon juice 1 tablespoon cooking oil ½ teaspoon dried thyme, crushed 4 ounces thinly sliced fully cooked ham	● In a small mixing bowl combine lemon juice, the 1 tablespoon cooking oil, and thyme. Remove top piece of plastic wrap; rub lemon mixture over top surface of turkey with your fingers. Place slices of ham evenly on top of turkey.
1 large tomato, peeled, seeded, and chopped 2 tablespoons grated Parmesan cheese	● Sprinkle with the chopped tomato and Parmesan cheese. Starting from narrow end, tightly roll up turkey, jelly-roll style. Tie turkey roll together securely with cord. Cover and chill, if desired.
Cooking oil	● Insert meat thermometer near center of turkey roll. In a covered grill arrange preheated coals around a drip pan; test for *medium* heat above pan. Place turkey roll on grill rack over drip pan but not over coals. Brush with the additional cooking oil. Lower grill hood. Grill for 1 to 1¼ hours or till meat thermometer registers 185°. Makes 6 to 8 servings.
	● **Rotisserie method:** Insert a spit rod lengthwise through center of turkey roll. Adjust holding forks; test balance. Insert meat thermometer near center of turkey roll, not touching metal rod. Attach spit to grill; turn motor on. Grill turkey roll, on an uncovered grill, directly over *medium* coals for 1 to 1¼ hours or till meat thermometer registers 185°.

MENU COUNTDOWN
One day ahead:
Cook vegetables and prepare marinade for Cauliflower 'n' Tomato Toss; cover and marinate vegetables in refrigerator. Clean and refrigerate lettuce.
    Prepare Raspberry Chantilly.
Several hours ahead:
Shape Turkey-Ham Roll; cover and refrigerate.
    For chantilly in molds without holes, invert onto paper towels and chill.
One hour and 45 minutes ahead:
Light charcoal in grill.
One hour and 15 minutes ahead:
Start grilling Turkey-Ham Roll.
20 minutes ahead:
Remove dessert from molds; garnish. Chill.
    Toss salad together and pour drinks.

Boning a turkey breast is much like boning a chicken breast. Place the turkey half breast, bone side down, onto a cutting board. Press the flat side of a knife blade against the rib bones and use a sawing motion to cut the meat away. If necessary, use your other hand to gently pull the meat away as you cut it from the bones. Discard the bones.

Cauliflower 'n' Tomato Toss

Pictured on pages 72 and 73.

1 **small head cauliflower, cut into small flowerets**	● In a large saucepan on the range top cook the cauliflower flowerets, covered, in a small amount of boiling salted water for 12 minutes or till nearly tender; drain. Place the cooked cauliflower, cherry tomatoes, and green pepper in a bowl.
1 **cup cherry tomatoes, halved**	
½ **cup chopped green pepper**	

Make this salad completely ahead by washing and tearing the lettuce when you assemble the marinated vegetables. Then store the lettuce in a plastic bag in the refrigerator overnight.

¾ **cup white wine vinegar**
½ **cup salad oil**
¼ **cup sugar**
1 **tablespoon snipped fresh basil *or* 1 teaspoon dried basil, crushed**
1 **teaspoon salt**
⅛ **teaspoon pepper**
1 **small head lettuce, torn into bite-size pieces (about 6 cups)**

● For marinade, place vinegar, salad oil, sugar, basil, salt, and pepper in a screw-top jar; cover and shake till well combined. Pour over vegetable mixture in the bowl. Cover and marinate in the refrigerator overnight, spooning marinade over vegetables several times.

To serve, drain vegetables, reserving ¼ cup marinade. Place the marinated vegetables in a large salad bowl. Add torn lettuce and the reserved marinade; toss gently. Makes 6 to 8 servings.

Raspberry Chantilly

6 *or* 8 **six-inch squares cheesecloth**
1 **8-ounce package cream cheese, softened**
½ **teaspoon vanilla**
½ **cup sifted powdered sugar**
1 **cup whipping cream**
2½ **cups fresh *or* frozen (thawed) raspberries**
¼ **cup water**
2 **tablespoons sugar**
2 **teaspoons cornstarch**

● Moisten cheesecloth till just damp. Line six ½-cup *or* eight ⅓-cup molds each with one damp cheesecloth square, allowing cheesecloth to hang over edges.

In a large mixer bowl beat cream cheese and vanilla together with an electric mixer till combined. Gradually add powdered sugar, beating till fluffy. In another bowl, beat cream to soft peaks; fold into cheese mixture. Spoon mixture into molds. Cover; chill several hours.

For sauce, press the 2½ cups raspberries through a sieve to remove seeds. In a saucepan combine the raspberry pulp and juice, water, sugar, and cornstarch. Cook and stir till bubbly. Cook 2 minutes more; cover and chill.

To serve the *Raspberry Chantilly,* spoon the sauce over each unmolded dessert and garnish with fresh raspberries and a sprig of mint.

Fresh raspberries
Fresh mint sprigs

● Invert molds without holes onto paper towels, leaving molds and cheesecloth intact; chill several hours. Transfer to plates. For coeur à la crème molds (molds with holes), invert onto plates just before serving.

Lift off molds; peel off cheesecloth. Spoon sauce over each dessert; garnish with raspberries and mint, as shown at right. Makes 6 or 8 servings.

Mesquite-Smoked Beef Roast

4 to 6 mesquite wood chunks	● At least one hour before smoke-cooking, soak wood chunks in enough water to cover.
1 4-pound beef rib roast **Whole black peppercorns**	● Using a long-tine fork, make 1-inch-deep holes, spaced ¾ inch apart, in the surface of the fat side of the roast; insert a whole peppercorn into each hole. Close holes by rubbing the fat surface of the roast with the smooth edge of the long-tine fork.
1½ teaspoons Worcestershire sauce **½ teaspoon seasoned salt** **½ teaspoon celery salt**	● In a custard cup combine Worcestershire sauce, seasoned salt, and celery salt. Rub the mixture over the surface of the roast with your fingers. Insert a meat thermometer near the center of the roast, not touching bone.
	● *Grill method:* Drain wood chunks. In a covered grill arrange preheated coals around drip pan; test for *medium* heat above pan. Pour 1 inch of water into drip pan. Place drained wood chunks on top of the preheated coals. Place roast, fat side up, on grill rack over drip pan but not over coals. Lower grill hood. Grill till meat thermometer registers 140° for rare (about 2 hours), 160° for medium (about 2¼ hours), and 170° for well-done (about 2½ hours), adding more water when necessary.
	● *Smoker method:* Drain the wood chunks. In a water smoker arrange preheated coals, drained wood chunks, and water pan in smoker according to the manufacturer's directions; pour water into pan. Place roast, fat side up, on grill rack over water pan. Lower smoker hood. Grill till meat thermometer registers 140° for rare (about 3 hours), 160° for medium (about 3½ hours), and 170° for well-done (about 4 hours). Makes 8 servings.

When our home economists tested this recipe, it had a wonderful smoky flavor. Depending on your taste, you can boost or play down that flavor by using either more or less wood. If you're planning to serve the beef cold, keep in mind that a smoke flavor is more pronounced in cold foods.

The Secret to Smoke-Cooking

Take the ho-hum out of ordinary steak, chicken, and fish by discovering the delicious outdoor, smoky flavor that wood chips or chunks can add.

Start with one type of wood. Then experiment with combinations of different wood.

Hickory, an ever-so-popular wood, will add an intense, sweet flavor to barbecued foods.

For a light, clean, smoky flavor, try mesquite. It is also available in a charcoal briquette form.

When you prefer a delicately sweet smoke, try using apple, cherry, or Osage orange wood.

Be sure to use only those woods from either fruit or nut trees. Soft woods, such as evergreens, will discolor the food and give it a bitter taste.

At least one hour before smoke-cooking, soak the wood in water. This will cause the chips or chunks to smolder rather than flame when you add them to the hot coals.

Sugar Smoked Pork Ribs

1 lemon, cut in half
4 pounds pork spareribs
1 to 2 tablespoons soy
    sauce
	● Squeeze and rub the cut surface of the lemon halves over the ribs. Then rub soy sauce over the ribs with your fingers.
	    Cover and let ribs stand in the refrigerator for 1 hour.

4 cups wood chips *or* 10 to **12 wood chunks** **(hickory *or* Osage** **orange)**	● At least one hour before smoke-cooking, soak 4 cups of wood chips (for the grill method) or 10 to 12 wood chunks (for the smoker method) in enough water to cover.
	● *Grill method:* Drain wood chips. In a covered grill arrange preheated coals around drip pan; test for *medium* heat above pan. Pour 1 inch of water into drip pan. Sprinkle *one-fourth* (about 1 cup) of the drained chips over the preheated coals. Place ribs in a rib rack, if desired. Place ribs on grill rack over drip pan but not over coals. Lower grill hood. Grill for 1 hour, adding more dampened chips every 15 minutes and more water when necessary.
	● *Smoker method:* Drain wood chunks. In a water smoker arrange preheated coals, drained wood chunks, and water pan in the smoker according to manufacturer's directions; pour water into pan. Place ribs in a rib rack, if desired. Place ribs on grill rack over water pan. Lower smoker hood. Grill for 3¾ hours.
¼ cup packed brown sugar	● Sprinkle the ribs with the brown sugar. Lower grill or smoker hood. Grill about 15 minutes more or till meat pulls away from bone (meat may still be pink). To serve, cut ribs into serving-size pieces. Makes 4 to 6 servings.

Smoke-cooking on the grill or in a smoker adds flavor to food but doesn't preserve it. To be safe, make sure to eat the ribs while they're still hot, and refrigerate any leftovers.

Covered Grills

A DOUBLE-DUTY APPLIANCE!

Here's another use for your covered grill—smoke-cooking. Read on and we'll show you how to convert it into a smoker.

First start by soaking a couple of handfuls of wood chips in water for about one hour. (Refer to the tip on page 77 in choosing which type of wood to use.) Then preheat the coals and arrange them around an empty drip pan. Pour about 1 inch of water, wine, or fruit juice into the pan. Sprinkle the hot coals with some of the wet wood chips. Then place the grill rack about 6 inches above the coals and set the meat on it, as shown at right. Check the grill every 15 to 25 minutes. Don't let the drip pan go dry. Add more liquid, if necessary. Also add more charcoal and dampened wood chips as needed to maintain an even cooking temperature and a steady flow of smoke.

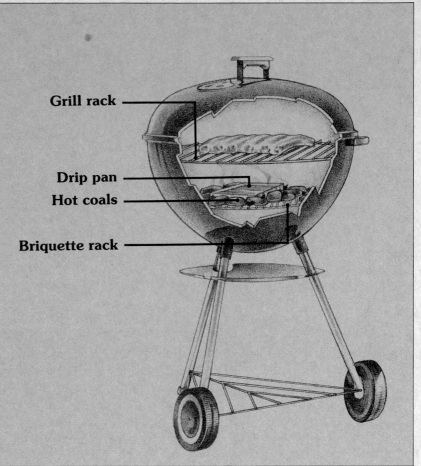

Grill rack

Drip pan

Hot coals

Briquette rack

Smokers

A SPECIAL TYPE OF GRILL!

Water smokers are unique grills especially designed for smoke-cooking. Their shape allows slightly better circulation of heat and steam around the food than in a regular covered grill.

A popular style is the charcoal dome, as shown at right. Smokers can also be heated by gas or electricity. Be sure to read the manufacturer's instructions to understand how to use your model.

Although all charcoal domes are not exactly alike, the basic procedure is the same. Once the coals are heated, place the wet wood chunks on top. Then place the meat on the grill rack. Some smokers have additional grill racks so different foods can be cooked simultaneously. Keep the food moist while it cooks by filling the water pan with water, wine, or fruit juice. After a couple of hours, check to see if you need to add more charcoal, dampened wood chunks, or liquid.

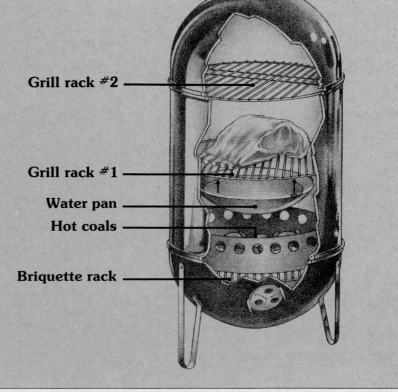

Grill rack #2

Grill rack #1

Water pan

Hot coals

Briquette rack

Curry-Stuffed Smoked Capon

1 cup chopped onion
1 cup chopped celery
4 teaspoons curry powder
1 teaspoon salt
¼ teaspoon pepper
¼ cup butter *or* margarine
6 cups firm-texture dry
   bread cubes (see tip,
   far right)
⅔ cup apple juice *or* cider

● For stuffing, in a saucepan on the range top cook onion, celery, curry powder, salt, and pepper in butter or margarine till vegetables are tender but not brown. Remove from heat and stir in the dry bread cubes. Add apple juice or cider and toss to mix well. Cover and chill till time to stuff the bird.

The secret to the deliciously moist curry dressing is to use firm-texture dry bread cubes— they keep the dressing from becoming too wet. To make the firm-texture dry bread cubes, place approximately 9 cups *fresh bread cubes* in a shallow baking pan and toast in a 325° oven for 15 to 20 minutes or till dry.

8 cups wood chips

● At least one hour before smoke-cooking, soak wood chips in enough water to cover.

1 5- to 7-pound capon *or*
   whole roasting chicken

● Meanwhile, rinse the capon or roasting chicken; pat excess moisture from bird with paper towels.
   Spoon some of the stuffing mixture into the neck cavity. Skewer neck skin to back of bird. Lightly spoon the stuffing into body cavity; do not pack. Tie the legs to tail with cord. Twist the wing tips under back. Insert a meat thermometer in the center of the inside thigh muscle, not touching bone.

● Place any remaining stuffing in center of a piece of *heavy* foil; bring up the long edges of the foil and, leaving a little space for the expansion of steam, seal tightly with a double fold. Then fold short ends to seal.

Cooking oil

● Drain wood chips. In a covered grill arrange preheated coals around drip pan; test for *medium-slow* heat above pan. Pour 1 inch of water into drip pan. Sprinkle *one-fourth* (about 2 cups) of the drained chips over preheated coals. Place the stuffed bird, breast side up, on the grill rack over drip pan but not over coals. Brush bird with cooking oil. Lower grill hood. Grill for 2½ to 2¾ hours or till meat thermometer registers 185°, adding more dampened chips and brushing bird with oil every 30 minutes.

Don't be fooled! Smoke-cooked food may still look a little pink after it is fully cooked. Use an accurate meat thermometer to be sure that poultry or large pieces of meat are done.

● Place the foil packet of stuffing on the grill rack with bird during the last 30 to 45 minutes of grilling. Serves 6 to 8.

Swiss Smoked Trout

2 **cups wood chips** 4 **fresh *or* frozen pan-dressed lake *or* brook trout, *or* perch (about 8 ounces each)**	● At least one hour before smoke-cooking, soak the wood chips in enough water to cover. Thaw fish, if frozen.
2 **slices bacon** ½ **cup chopped fresh mushrooms** 2 **tablespoons sliced green onion**	● Meanwhile, for filling, in a skillet on the range top cook bacon till crisp. Drain, reserving 1 tablespoon fat. Crumble bacon; set aside. In the skillet cook mushrooms and onion in the reserved fat till onion is tender but not brown. Remove from heat and stir in the cooked bacon.
¼ **cup shredded Swiss cheese (1 ounce)** 1 **tablespoon butter *or* margarine, melted**	● Spoon *one-fourth* of the filling into *each* of the fish cavities. Add *1* tablespoon of Swiss cheese to *each* cavity. Skewer the cavity opening closed with wooden toothpicks. Brush fish with melted butter or margarine.
	● *Grill method:* Drain wood chips. In a covered grill arrange the preheated coals around the drip pan; test for *medium* heat above pan. Pour 1 inch of water into drip pan. Sprinkle the drained chips over the preheated coals. Place the fish on the grill rack over drip pan but not over coals. Lower grill hood. Grill for 20 to 25 minutes or till fish flakes easily when tested with a fork.
	● *Smoker method:* Drain wood chips. In a water smoker arrange preheated coals, drained wood chips, and water pan in smoker according to manufacturer's directions; pour water into pan. Place fish on grill rack over water pan. Lower smoker hood. Grill for 20 to 25 minutes or till fish flakes easily when tested with a fork. Makes 4 servings.

Having trouble with wood chips floating while you're trying to soak them in water? Put a plate on top to hold them down.

Green-Tomato Chutney
(see recipe, page 85)

Mustard Relish
(see recipe, page 84)

Curried Fruit Relish

1 8-ounce can crushed
   pineapple (juice pack)
¼ cup packed brown sugar
2 tablespoons vinegar
½ teaspoon curry powder
⅛ teaspoon garlic powder
2 large unripe pears, peeled,
   cored, and chopped

● In a medium saucepan combine the *undrained* pineapple, brown sugar, vinegar, curry powder, and garlic powder. On the range top, bring to boiling; add pears. Simmer, uncovered, for 6 to 8 minutes or till fruit is tender and relish is the desired consistency.

Store relish, in a tightly covered container, in the refrigerator for up to 2 months. Serve with meat or poultry. Makes 1¾ cups.

This easy fruit combo looks and tastes like chutney. Use slightly underripe pears for a chunky texture.

Jiffy Pickles

1 tablespoon mixed
   pickling spice
¾ cup vinegar
½ cup sugar
½ teaspoon salt
¼ teaspoon ground turmeric
4 cups desired vegetables
   (such as zucchini or
   cucumber slices; small
   onion rings; and/or
   carrot sticks)

● Tie the mixed pickling spice in a piece of cheesecloth.

In a saucepan combine the pickling spice bag, vinegar, sugar, salt, and turmeric. On the range top, bring to boiling; reduce heat. Simmer for 5 minutes. Remove from heat; pour over the desired vegetables. Cool mixture to room temperature.

Store pickles, in a tightly covered container, in the refrigerator for up to 2 weeks. Remove spice bag before serving. Makes 4 cups.

These pickles definitely live up to their name. Just pour the pickling brine over the fresh vegetables and let steep overnight— then enjoy!

Curried Fruit Relish

Zippy Onion Relish

Honey Applesauce

8	medium cooking apples, peeled, cored, and cut up
½	cup water
1	tablespoon honey
1	tablespoon lemon juice

● In a medium saucepan combine apples, water, honey, and lemon juice. On the range top, bring to boiling; reduce heat. Simmer, covered, for 8 to 10 minutes or till apples are tender. Mash apples slightly.

Store applesauce, in a tightly covered container, in the refrigerator for up to 1 week. Makes 2½ cups.

Honey-sweet applesauce is great on franks, pork chops, or chicken. Or, sprinkle cinnamon on top and serve it as a simple dessert.

Zippy Onion Relish

3	large onions, chopped
½	cup tomato sauce
3	tablespoons catsup
2	tablespoons water
1½	teaspoons sugar
½	teaspoon dried oregano, crushed
¼	teaspoon salt
¼	teaspoon garlic salt
¼	teaspoon crushed red pepper

● In a medium saucepan combine the chopped onions, tomato sauce, catsup, water, sugar, oregano, salt, garlic salt, and red pepper. On the range top, bring to boiling; reduce heat. Simmer, covered, about 20 minutes or till the onions are just tender.

Store relish, in a tightly covered container, in the refrigerator for up to 2 weeks. Makes 2½ cups.

Take the routine out of franks, sausages, and hamburgers with this hot and spicy relish.

Mustard Relish

Pictured on pages 82 and 83.

3 cups water
3 cups finely chopped cabbage
3 cups finely chopped cucumber
1 cup finely chopped green pepper
1 cup finely chopped celery
¾ cup finely chopped onion
½ cup chopped pimiento
⅓ cup pickling salt
1¼ cups vinegar
⅔ cup sugar
⅔ cup water
2 tablespoons mustard seed

● In a large mixing bowl combine the 3 cups water, cabbage, cucumber, green pepper, celery, onion, pimiento, and pickling salt; toss to mix thoroughly. Let mixture stand for 3 hours. Drain; rinse well with cold water and drain again.

In a saucepan combine vinegar, sugar, the ⅔ cup water, and mustard seed. On the range top, bring to boiling; reduce heat. Simmer, uncovered, for 3 minutes. Add drained vegetables. Bring mixture to boiling again; reduce heat. Cook, uncovered, for 5 minutes more.

Ladle hot vegetables and syrup mixture into hot, clean pint jars, leaving ½-inch headspace. Wipe jar rims; adjust lids. Process in boiling water bath for 15 minutes (start timing when water boils). Makes 4 pints.

SNAP! You will sometimes hear this noise when the vacuum in the jar suddenly pulls the metal lid down as the jar cools, making a tight seal. Test for the seal by tapping the lid lightly with a metal spoon. A sealed jar with no food touching the lid has a clear ringing sound.

Steps to Home Canning

There's nothing tastier than home-canned relishes to add zest to your next barbecue. These easy-to-use canning steps will help you turn out perfect pickled vegetable and fruit relishes every time.

1 Set the canner with its rack on the range and fill it with four to five inches of water. Cover and start heating the water over high heat. In another kettle heat additional water.

2 While the water is heating, follow the recipe directions for cooking the relish. When the relish is finished cooking and the water in the canner is simmering, fill hot, clean pint jars with the hot relish; leave a ½-inch space between the top of the food and the rim of the jar. With a damp cloth, wipe off the rim of the jar to remove any food particles. Follow the package directions for preparing the metal sealing lids. Place the lid on the jar so that the sealing compound rests on the rim. Screw on the metal bands.

3 Using a jar lifter, place the jars on the rack in the canner.

4 When the last jar has been added, fill the canner with the additional heated water so that the water is one to two inches over jar tops. Bring the water in the canner to boiling. Start counting the processing time after the water comes to a boil. Adjust the heat so that the water will boil gently during the entire process.

5 When the processing time is up, turn the heat off. Use the jar lifter to transfer the hot jars to a rack in a draft-free area and let cool.

Green-Tomato Chutney

Pictured on pages 82 and 83.

4 pounds green tomatoes,
  cored and cut up
  (10 to 14 tomatoes)
2 medium sweet red *or*
  green peppers, seeded
  and cut up
2 medium pears, peeled,
  cored, and cut up
1 medium onion, cut up
1½ cups vinegar
1⅓ cups sugar
2 teaspoons dry mustard
1 teaspoon salt
1 cup raisins *or* dried
  currants

● Using a food processor or the coarse blade of a food grinder, chop or grind tomatoes, red or green peppers, pears, and onion (should measure 10 cups).

In a large saucepan combine the chopped mixture, vinegar, sugar, dry mustard, and salt. On the range top, bring to boiling, stirring to dissolve sugar; reduce heat. Cover; boil gently for 10 minutes. Uncover; stir in raisins or dried currants. Cook, uncovered, for 35 minutes. Ladle hot relish into hot, clean pint jars, leaving ½-inch headspace. Wipe jar rims; adjust lids. Process in boiling water bath for 10 minutes (start timing when water boils). Makes 4 pints.

Living closer to the clouds requires some cooking adjustments. If you live at a high altitude, you'll need to allow more time for foods to heat through. Add 1 minute to the water-bath processing time for each 1,000 feet that you live above sea level.

Citrus Chutney

3 large oranges
1½ cups packed brown sugar
1 medium onion, chopped
½ cup raisins
¼ cup lemon juice
¼ cup lime juice
1 tablespoon grated
  gingerroot
1 teaspoon salt
½ teaspoon ground
  cinnamon
½ teaspoon ground allspice
¼ teaspoon ground cloves
½ cup chopped almonds

● Peel oranges, reserving peel. Section oranges over a bowl to catch juices. Remove and discard the white membrane from the peel. Finely chop enough peel to make ¼ cup.

In a pan combine chopped orange peel, orange sections with juices, brown sugar, onion, raisins, lemon juice, lime juice, gingerroot, salt, cinnamon, allspice, and cloves. Bring to boiling. Add nuts; reduce heat. Boil gently, uncovered, for 30 minutes or till thickened, stirring occasionally. Cool. Store, tightly covered, in refrigerator. Makes about 2½ cups.

A variation of the Indian condiment, this chutney has a sweet, spicy, vinegary flavor. Serve *Citrus Chutney* with beef, pork, or poultry. If you have any leftover chutney, you can store it in the refrigerator for up to 2 months.

Virginia Corn

1 12-ounce can whole
  kernel corn
½ cup vinegar
¼ cup sugar
2 tablespoons chopped
  green pepper
1 tablespoon minced dried
  onion
½ teaspoon salt
¼ teaspoon celery seed
¼ teaspoon mustard seed
¼ teaspoon bottled hot
  pepper sauce
1 tablespoon chopped
  pimiento

● In a saucepan combine the *undrained* whole kernel corn, vinegar, sugar, chopped green pepper, minced dried onion, salt, celery seed, mustard seed, and bottled hot pepper sauce.

On the range top, bring mixture to boiling, stirring occasionally; reduce heat. Boil gently, uncovered, for 2 minutes. Remove from heat and stir in the chopped pimiento. Transfer to a covered container and chill till serving time. Makes 1½ cups.

Cooks down South relish good times and good food. One of their favorites is this colorful, peppery-hot relish that can be served either as a condiment or side dish.

Tomato-Rice Cups

3 large tomatoes

● For cups, cut tomatoes in half. Scoop out the seeds and pulp from *each* tomato half, leaving a ¼-inch-thick shell. Discard seeds. Chop pulp; set aside. Invert shells onto paper towels to drain.

2 tablespoons sliced
almonds
2 tablespoons plain yogurt
¼ teaspoon salt
Dash garlic powder
1 tablespoon butter *or*
margarine, softened
¾ cup loosely packed
spinach
1 cup cooked rice

● In a mixing bowl combine the sliced almonds, yogurt, salt, and garlic powder. Add the softened butter or margarine; mix together well.

Finely chop the spinach. Stir the chopped spinach, cooked rice, and chopped tomato into the yogurt mixture.

● Spoon about ¼ *cup* of rice mixture into *each* tomato shell. Cut four 8-inch-square pieces of *heavy* foil. Wrap *each* filled tomato shell in a piece of foil.

Grill, on an uncovered grill, directly over *medium* coals for 20 to 25 minutes or till heated through. Makes 6 servings.

Make these attractive tomato cups by first cutting the tomatoes in half with a sharp knife.

Then use a spoon to scoop out the center of *each* tomato half, leaving a ¼-inch-thick shell.

Spoon about ¼ *cup* of the rice mixture into each tomato shell and wrap in a piece of *heavy* foil.

Garden Cups

2 small tomatoes Salt Pepper	● For tomato cups, cut a small slice from the top of each tomato. Use a spoon to scoop out the seeds and pulp from *each* tomato, leaving a ¼-inch-thick shell. Discard the seeds. Chop the pulp and set pulp aside. Invert shells onto paper towels to drain. 　Sprinkle the inside of *each* tomato shell lightly with salt and pepper.	**When it's up to you to think of something great to serve, choose these tomato cups filled with herbed peas. To cut 5 to 10 minutes off of the cooking time, grill the wrapped tomato cups in a covered grill.**
2 teaspoons butter *or* margarine, melted 1 teaspoon snipped fresh basil *or* ¼ teaspoon dried basil, crushed ½ teaspoon minced dried onion ⅓ cup cooked peas	● For filling, in a small mixing bowl stir together melted butter or margarine, basil, and minced dried onion; toss with peas and the chopped tomato pulp.	
	● Spoon *half* of the pea mixture into *each* of the tomato shells. Cut two 8-inch-square pieces of *heavy* foil. Wrap *each* filled tomato shell in a piece of foil. 　Grill the wrapped tomato cups, on an uncovered grill, directly over *medium* coals for 20 to 25 minutes or till heated through. Makes 2 servings.	

Pilaf Peppers

1 cup quick-cooking rice ½ teaspoon finely shredded orange peel (set aside) 1 cup orange juice ¼ teaspoon salt	● Prepare the rice according to package directions, *except* substitute the orange juice for the water and use the ¼ teaspoon salt.	**When your foil-wrapped food doesn't need turning on the grill, bundle it in a piece of foil large enough to allow the sides to be drawn up around the food. To seal, twist the foil edges together at the top and press the twisted top down gently.**
¼ cup sliced green onion ¼ cup slivered almonds, toasted 2 teaspoons butter *or* margarine 2 large green peppers	● Stir green onion, toasted almonds, butter or margarine, and orange peel into the cooked rice. 　Remove tops from green peppers. Cut peppers in half lengthwise; remove seeds and membrane.	
	● Spoon *one-fourth* of the rice mixture into *each* of the green pepper shells. Cut four 14x12-inch pieces of *heavy* foil. Wrap *each* filled shell in a piece of foil. 　Grill the wrapped peppers, on an uncovered grill, directly over *medium* coals for 30 to 45 minutes or till heated through. Makes 4 servings.	

Barley-Stuffed Zucchini

4 medium zucchini	● Cut a thin, lengthwise slice off the bottom of each zucchini so it will sit flat. Cut a thin, lengthwise slice off the top of each zucchini. 　Use a spoon to scoop out the pulp from the center of *each* zucchini, leaving a ½-inch-thick shell. Chop the pulp and set aside.
Salt	● In a large skillet arrange the zucchini shells with top side down. On the range top, cook the zucchini shells, covered, in a small amount of boiling water for 3 to 5 minutes or till nearly tender; drain. 　Sprinkle the inside of each zucchini shell lightly with salt.
¼ cup chopped onion **1 small clove garlic, minced** **1 tablespoon butter *or* margarine** **1 beaten egg** **½ cup cooked barley *or* long grain rice** **¼ cup sunflower nuts** **¼ cup shredded cheddar cheese (1 ounce)**	● For the filling, in a medium saucepan on the range top cook the chopped zucchini, chopped onion, and minced garlic in butter or margarine till vegetables are tender but not brown. 　In a mixing bowl combine the beaten egg, cooked barley or long grain rice, sunflower nuts, and cheese. Add the cooked vegetable mixture and mix well.
2 teaspoons wheat germ	● Spoon *one-fourth* of the barley mixture into *each* of the zucchini shells and sprinkle with wheat germ. 　Make a 12-inch-square pan with *heavy* foil (see illustration on page 22); place the filled zucchini shells in the foil pan.
	● In a covered grill arrange preheated coals around the edge of the grill; test for *medium* heat above center of grill. Place foil pan containing the filled zucchini shells on the center of the grill rack but not over coals. Lower grill hood. Grill for 30 minutes or till heated through. Makes 6 to 8 servings.

Did your mom always have to remind you to "eat your vegetables"? Here's one vegetable that you'll want to dig into. Sunflower nuts and wheat germ add flavor and crunch to these fun-filled zucchini boats.

Lemony Green Beans

1 9-ounce package frozen
   cut green beans
½ teaspoon sugar
¼ teaspoon salt
   Dash pepper
3 thin lemon slices
½ cup sliced water
   chestnuts
½ small onion, cut into
   wedges and separated
   into pieces
1 tablespoon butter *or*
   margarine

● Partially thaw beans under hot running water about 30 seconds.

Cut a 14x12-inch piece of *heavy* foil. Place green beans in center of foil. Sprinkle with sugar, salt, and pepper. Top with the lemon slices, water chestnuts, and onion pieces. Dot with butter or margarine.

Bring up long edges of foil and, leaving a little space for expansion of steam, seal tightly with a double fold. Then fold short ends to seal.

Grill foil packet, on an uncovered grill, directly over *medium* coals for 15 minutes. Turn and grill for 15 to 20 minutes more or till beans are tender. Makes 4 servings.

On hot summer days, there's no need to spend a lot of time in a hot kitchen. You can cook your entire meal on the grill. Just wrap green beans, lemon slices, and water chestnuts in foil, and presto! You've got a delicious side dish.

Curried Stuffed Squash

1 cup water
¼ cup regular brown rice
¼ cup thinly sliced green onion
2 tablespoons raisins
1 teaspoon curry powder
½ teaspoon instant chicken bouillon granules
2 tablespoons coarsely chopped peanuts

● In a saucepan combine water, brown rice, thinly sliced green onion, raisins, curry powder, and instant chicken bouillon granules. On the range top, bring to boiling; reduce heat. Simmer, covered, for 45 to 55 minutes or till rice is tender and water is absorbed.
Remove from heat and stir in peanuts.

2 small acorn squash, cut in half (12 to 16 ounces each)

● Meanwhile, remove seeds from squash. Cut four 12-inch-square pieces of *heavy* foil. Wrap *each* squash half in a piece of foil. Grill squash, in a covered grill, directly over *medium* coals for 30 to 40 minutes or till tender.

● Remove squash from grill; unwrap. Spoon *one-fourth* of the rice mixture into the cavity of *each* piece of squash; rewrap squash in foil.
Grill stuffed squash, in a covered grill, directly over *medium* coals for 10 to 15 minutes or till squash is heated through. Makes 4 servings.

Serve either poultry or pork with this rice-filled squash, and you've got a complete meal. To add a decorative touch to the *Curried Stuffed Squash,* simply top it with a celery leaf and sprinkle with sliced green onion or peanuts.

Cheese 'n' Buttered Corn

1 5-ounce jar cheese spread with bacon
½ cup butter *or* margarine, softened
¼ teaspoon onion salt

● Place cheese spread, butter or margarine, and onion salt in a small mixer bowl. Beat with an electric mixer on medium speed till fluffy.

8 fresh ears of corn

● Remove husks and silk from corn.
Spread *each* ear of corn generously with the cheese mixture. Cut eight 12x8-inch pieces of *heavy* foil. Wrap *each* ear of corn in a piece of foil.
Grill corn, on an uncovered grill, directly over *medium-hot* coals for 20 to 25 minutes or till tender, turning often. Makes 8 servings.

If you're a peanut fan, try this nutty variation, Peanuts 'n' Buttered Corn. In a small mixing bowl stir together ½ cup *creamy peanut butter,* 2 tablespoons softened *butter or margarine,* ½ teaspoon *ground cinnamon,* and ⅛ teaspoon *bottled hot pepper sauce.* Spread on corn, wrap in foil, and grill as directed at left.

Vegetable Kabobs

Pictured on pages 4 and 5.

3 medium potatoes, quartered 1 10-ounce package frozen brussels sprouts	● In a covered saucepan on the range top, cook the potatoes in enough boiling salted water to cover for 10 minutes. Add brussels sprouts; bring the water back to boiling. Continue cooking the vegetables, covered, for 5 minutes more. Drain and cool slightly.
3 tablespoons olive oil *or* cooking oil 2 tablespoons lemon juice ½ teaspoon dried basil, crushed	● In a small mixing bowl combine olive oil or cooking oil, lemon juice, and basil.
1½ cups cherry tomatoes	● On six skewers alternately thread the potatoes, brussels sprouts, and cherry tomatoes. Place on a kabob rack, if desired. Brush kabobs with oil mixture. Grill kabobs, on an uncovered grill, directly over *medium* coals for 8 to 10 minutes or till heated through, turning often. Makes 6 servings.

Make full use of the hot coals by accompanying your favorite meat with *Vegetable Kabobs.* Place them around the edge of the grill during the last 8 minutes of cooking. Then, when the meat is finished, move the kabobs in toward the center for a minute or two, if necessary.

Cheesy Potato Boats

4 medium potatoes	● Scrub potatoes; prick several times with a fork. Cut four 6-inch-square pieces of *heavy* foil. Wrap *each* potato in a piece of foil. Grill potatoes, in a covered grill, directly over *medium-slow* coals for 1½ to 2 hours or till potatoes are tender.
½ of a 5-ounce jar cream cheese spread with pineapple (about ¼ cup) ¼ teaspoon salt Milk Paprika	● Unwrap potatoes and cut a lengthwise slice from the top of each potato; discard skin from the slice. Using a spoon, scoop out the insides of each potato, leaving ¼-inch-thick shell; set potato shells aside. In a mixing bowl mash the scooped-out potato and potato slice; stir in cheese spread and salt. Stir in enough milk (about 2 tablespoons) to make a stiff but fluffy consistency. Pile mashed potato mixture into the potato shells. Sprinkle with paprika.
	● Grill stuffed potato shells, in a covered grill, directly over *medium-slow* coals for 10 minutes or till potatoes are heated through. Makes 4 servings.

Let your microwave oven help you hurry-up the *Cheesy Potato Boats.* In a countertop microwave oven, arrange the scrubbed and pricked potatoes on a paper plate, leaving at least 1 inch between the potatoes. Micro-cook, uncovered, on 100% power (HIGH) till tender, allowing 13 to 15 minutes for four potatoes. Halfway through cooking time, rearrange and turn over potatoes. Then scoop out, fill, and grill the boats as directed at left.

Cheesy Garlic Bread

1 20-inch-long loaf French bread (3 to 4 inches in diameter)	● Slice the bread loaf into 1-inch diagonal slices, cutting to, but not through, the opposite side.
2 cloves garlic, minced **⅓ cup butter *or* margarine** **1 tablespoon finely snipped parsley**	● In a saucepan on the range top cook garlic in butter or margarine for 1 minute; stir in parsley. Brush *each* cut surface of bread with the butter mixture.

10 ¾-ounce slices American *or* Swiss cheese	● Cut cheese slices in half diagonally; insert *one* piece of cheese between *each* cut in bread loaf.
	    Cut a 28x18-inch piece of *heavy* foil. Place bread in center of foil. Bring up long edges of foil and, leaving a little space for expansion of steam, seal *loosely* with a double fold. Then fold short ends to seal.
	    Grill the wrapped bread, on an uncovered grill, directly over *slow* coals for 20 to 25 minutes or till heated through, turning frequently. Serves 10.

When you're in a hurry, you can assemble, wrap, and refrigerate this cheesy bread ahead of time. Then, about 25 minutes before serving, just put it on the grill.

Nutty-Fruit Kabobs

1 16-ounce jar spiced crab apples **1 tablespoon red raspberry *or* strawberry jelly** **¾ teaspoon cornstarch**	● Drain apples, reserving ¼ cup syrup. Set apples aside. For sauce, in a saucepan combine the reserved syrup, jelly, and cornstarch. On the range top, cook and stir till thickened and bubbly. Cook and stir for 2 minutes more.
½ of a 3-ounce package cream cheese, softened **1 tablespoon honey** **¼ of a 10¾-ounce frozen loaf pound cake, thawed and cut into 1-inch cubes** **⅓ cup chopped peanuts** **1 medium banana, bias-sliced into 1-inch slices** **1 tablespoon lemon juice**	● In a small mixing bowl stir together cream cheese and honey. Spread cheese mixture lightly on *two opposite sides* of each cake cube. Dip cheese sides of cake cubes into chopped peanuts. Lightly toss the banana slices with the lemon juice.
	● On four skewers alternately thread apples, cake, and banana slices. Grill, on an uncovered grill, directly over *medium* coals for 5 minutes, turning often. Serve with sauce. Serves 4.

Don't let your grill-top repertoire stop with main dishes. End your barbecued dinner with something extra good from the grill such as these *Nutty-Fruit Kabobs*.

Potato Skins

4 medium potatoes	● Scrub potatoes; prick several times with a fork. Wrap *each* potato in one 6-inch-square piece of *heavy* foil. 　Grill potatoes, in a covered grill, directly over *medium-slow* coals for 1½ to 2 hours or till tender. 　Unwrap potatoes; quarter lengthwise. Scoop out insides, leaving ¼-inch-thick shells. Use insides for another purpose.
	● Grill skins, skin side down, on an uncovered grill over *medium-slow* coals for 5 minutes or till crisp. Continue as directed below with desired seasoning variation. Makes 16 potato skins.
½ cup shredded cheddar 　　cheese (2 ounces) **½ cup sour cream dip 　　with French onion** **4 slices bacon, cooked and 　　crumbled**	● **Sour Cream 'n' Onion Skins:** Top potato skins with cheese; grill for 2 to 3 minutes more or till cheese melts. 　Top with sour cream dip and sprinkle with crumbled bacon.
¼ cup butter *or* 　　margarine, melted **3 tablespoons grated 　　Parmesan cheese** **¼ teaspoon garlic powder 　　Dash paprika**	● **Parmesan Skins:** Combine butter or margarine, Parmesan cheese, and garlic powder; brush over top of potato skins. 　Grill for 2 to 3 minutes more or till heated through. Sprinkle with paprika.
1 teaspoon curry powder **3 tablespoons butter *or* 　　margarine** **2 tablespoons finely 　　chopped peanuts**	● **Curried Skins:** In a pan on the range top cook curry powder in butter for 5 minutes; brush over top of skins. 　Sprinkle with nuts. Grill for 2 to 3 minutes more or till heated through.

Make potato skins by first cutting the baked potatoes lengthwise into quarters.

Using a spoon, scoop out the inside of the potato, leaving ¼-inch-thick shell.

Sprinkle one or a variety of these toppings on the potato skins.

Take your pick of Curried, Sour Cream 'n' Onion, or Parmesan Potato Skins. They make a great opener for almost any cookout.

Index

Tips